TO BE
DISPOSED
BY
AUTHORITY

D0294775

MUGGERIDGE ANCIENT AND MODERN

MUGGERIDGE
Ancient & Modern

Malcolm Muggeridge

Edited by
Christopher Ralling and Jane Bywaters
With drawings by Trog

BRITISH BROADCASTING CORPORATION

Acknowledgement is due to the following for permission to reproduce photographs: British Library of Political and Economic Science (Beatrice and Sidney Webb); Paul Popper Ltd (Kerala and Simla); BBC (Empire Loyalists, Leonard Woolf); Terence Spencer/Colorific! (Alice); BBC Hulton Picture Library (P. G. Wodehouse); Keystone Press Agency Ltd (Editor of Punch); Rex Features Ltd (Coco Chanel).

Published by the
British Broadcasting Corporation
35 Marylebone High Street, London W1M 4AA

First published 1967 as *Muggeridge through the Microphone*
This edition first published 1981
© Malcolm Muggeridge 1966, 1967, 1981
ISBN 0 563 17905 8

Printed in England
by Whitstable Litho Limited, Whitstable, Kent

Contents

If, on the judgement day, I was confronted with God and I found that God took Himself seriously, I would ask to go to the other place.

Foreword

Shakespeare makes Macbeth complain bitterly when, after he has arranged for Banquo to be murdered, he turns up as a ghost at a banquet in Macbeth's honour:

> . . . . the time has been
> That when the brains were out the man would die,
> And there an end; but now they rise again.

In the same sort of way, tapes and film nowadays preserve words and postures which might otherwise be assumed to have been mercifully lost for ever. When I first started holding forth in public – at a scandalously early age, in support of my father's candidature in municipal and parliamentary elections – it never so much as occurred to me that my words, once uttered, would be other than like puffs of smoke, briefly existing, and then dispersed. Later, when I started earning my living by writing in newspapers and magazines, now some half a century ago, I assumed that the words I wrote would last no longer than the brief lives of the publications in which they appeared. Even out at Colindale, where magazines and newspapers are stored and catalogued for reference purposes, I was given to understand that the ever-growing accumulation of printed matter there had a term set to its existence, as the paper itself was fated in due course to disintegrate. 'Dust to dust,' I reflected sententiously. 'O printed word, where is thy sting?'

With the invention of microfilm, this is no longer the case; written words can last for ever, as spoken ones can be heard as and when required till the end of time. The Tower of Babel is thus immortalised, and all our scribble made available through the ages, so that instead of an author's collected works, the dread prospect arises of his collected words. A minuscule portent in this respect was the publication in 1967

11

by the BBC, under the kindly auspices of Christopher Ralling, of a collection of my own utterances on radio and television, embellished by that excellent artist, Trog, and entitled
Muggeridge Through the Microphone. Now, to bring the collection up to date, the deposit of the intervening fourteen years
has been sifted for pay-dirt in the way of scripts, broadcasts,
wisecracks and other odds-and-ends culled from the arc-
hives, with additional Trog drawings, and taking the same
title – *Muggeridge: Ancient and Modern* – as a series of TV
programmes put together by Jonathan Stedall from old footage, enlivened by comment thereon. I must say I find the title
pleasing – better to be a hymn than just a him.

The task of selecting suitable items to add to the original book was undertaken by Jane Bywaters. How my heart
went out to her when I thought of her looking hour after
hour, at microfilm, and listening to my untuneful voice pon-
tificating! However, she was kind enough to say that her
listening hours passed amusingly, and certainly the result
justified her assiduity. Naturally, she drew heavily on that
old favourite, *Any Questions?*, a seemingly indestructible
programme of which my memories as a participant go back
so far that I wonder whether there was ever a time when it
was not a regular Friday offering. Changes have, of course,
taken place; in its early days of innocence there used to be on
the panel a certified *Any Questions?* countryman, who would
confute the more sophisticated panelists by remarking in a
rich west-country dialect that in his experience there was
nothing like pig-shit for bringing on the crops. Nowadays,
the certified countryman has gone, to be replaced by balanc-
ing politicians who hurl bromides at one another in the most
spirited manner; and the homely humour of Mary Stocks –
alas, deceased – has given place to fiery actresses, Vanessa
Redgraves of the provinces. All the same, the good old programme goes on, and has yielded up its *pensées* to Jane Bywaters. I was particularly glad to have preserved my apocalyptic
vision of seeing in the nuclear holocaust on an *Any Questions?* programme, and hearing, as the mushroom clouds
formed, a life-peeress with a moustache insisting that what is

needed to deal with juvenile delinquency is more and better education.

Then, of course, there are the interviews, all patiently explored. My own memories, both of interviewing and being interviewed, are dim. Was it Wednesday or Saturday Parkinson? David or Jonathan Dimbleby? And then the other way round, face to face and knee to knee with a bishop; the camera zooming in, red-eyed, the floor-manager's arm raised – 'Bishop, is there an after-life?', when he was expecting something easy like: 'Bishop, why is church attendance falling off?' Sydney Smith speaks of being preached to death by wild curates. What would he think today of being interviewed to death by repetitive questions? It sometimes seems nowadays as though the interviewers outnumber the interviewees, who, passed from programme to programme, get battered and soiled, like much-used playing cards. I was glad Jane Bywaters salvaged the interview with the young clergyman who nourished the ambition to be a truthful gossip-writer – like hoping to be a sedentary acrobat or a chaste whore.

Also at her disposal were the exchanges between Jonathan Stedall and myself in the cutting-room as we looked at old footage together – mostly in black-and-white, incidentally, and confirming my opinion that all technological advances are retrograde. It was the strangest of situations – I as myself, looking at another self on a screen, and appraising this other self's performance. As a form of torture, it was something that Torquemada in the heyday of the Inquisition would have been glad to know more about. Could it really be me – this attitudinising, opinionated alter ego or *doppelgänger*? Clearly yes, and then again, clearly no.

In the days when I used to look at television, before I had my aerials removed, I was prone to fall asleep in front of the screen. This happens to viewers; it is by no means uncommon to see on a summer's evening a whole family gathered round their television set and quietly sleeping. To sleep, and then perchance to dream – ah, there's the rub, as Hamlet puts it. On one such occasion, waking and blinking, sleepy-eyed, into the screen, I saw on it some posturing fool who filled me with particular distaste, and then, appalled, realised that it was, or purported to be, myself. Or was it just Mike Yarwood being me? Or my waxwork from Madame Tussaud's Exhibition out on a spree?

Brooding on this macabre experience, I decided that the camera, with all its sins of omission and commission, might surely be used for this one good purpose – to let the drunkard see and hear what a repetitive bore he is in his cups, the lecher how unlike Abelard when on seduction bent, the orator how uncompelling on the rostrum. What a help it would be to the priest hearing confessions if he could arrange for the penitent to see himself committing his sins! How humbling for the professor and the politician if they found themselves sitting with their audiences instead of confronting them! Even for dear Trog, a lesson – that the caricature is veritably the man.

The original selection, I should add, was made largely by Christopher Ralling, whose idea this book was and to whose enterprise its appearance was due. If it deserves a dedication it should be to him and Jane Bywaters, and to Tony Kingsford of BBC Publications, who put it together and supervised its publication.

Malcolm Muggeridge

Introduction

St Augustine, looking back in his Confessions on his time as a professor of rhetoric, scornfully described himself as a vendor of words. I, too, have earned my living by selling words, but prefer to call myself a communicator. In my earliest recollections I see myself holding forth to whoever would listen just for the delight of so doing, and I distinctly remember turning over the pages of books and newspapers when their contents were still largely mysterious. Already, it seems, the twentieth-century obsession with communication as an end rather than a means had taken hold of me. I was a disciple of Marshall McLuhan long before he had propounded his famous dictum that the medium is the message.

Thus radio, and later television, came to pass in my eyes as naturally and inevitably as sea navigation in the eyes of a Vasco da Gama, or internal combustion in the eyes of a Henry Ford. I saw nothing to marvel at in them; even now I find it difficult to think of them as having been deliberately invented. When mankind became possessed with a passion to move, lo! there was a wheel. Likewise, when they were possessed with a passion to communicate, lo! there were words. The wheel in due course became jet propulsion, supersonic flight, astronautics; the words were projected by rotary press, microphone, video-tape. Yet movement and communication remained the essential purpose. In other words, those two characteristic pursuits of our time – speed and mass-communications – are not to be regarded as something devised to make or mar our way of life. Rather, they are an emanation of it. If, as may well prove to be the case, they come to be seen historically as having brought about the destruction of our civilisation, it will not be because of some malign impulse or force outside ourselves. We shall have done the job with our own hopes and desires – Prometheus tearing out his own entrails, gouging out his own eyes.

For me conscious communication began with print. What a moment that was in one's life when for the first time a limp, damp galley was laid on one's desk to be corrected, the ink running into little black rivulets as one attempted to write corrections on it! Empty words, no doubt, about some long forgotten issue, but read the next morning with such inordinate pride. Subsequently, there have been miles and miles of galleys, enough to encircle the globe; a preposterous paper-chase through the mists and swamps of troubled years.

I cannot pretend that my first acquaintance with broadcasting generated any comparable excitement. Written words, however evanescent, do briefly exist, like fireflies; spoken ones disappear as soon as they are uttered, carried away on the invisible waves of sound. Nowadays, of course, there is tape to preserve them, but only, surely, the most narcissistic or portentous temperament would incline one to listen to one's own past broadcasts. Even so, the broadcasting scene remains unforgettable – the airless, sultry studio; the little red light indicating that one is on the air; the flashing green light telling one to start or stop, to slow down or speed up; the inexorably moving hand of the noiseless clock; the figures behind the glass partition, so near and yet so remote; the glass of water always brackish to the taste; the sense of being far, far away from everyone and everything, in total isolation. How can I ever forget it?

The first broadcast I ever gave was on Sidney and Beatrice Webb. I have totally forgotten how I came to give it and what I said, but it must have caused offence because I received a letter from George Barnes – a bizarre but rather attractive ex-naval officer then bearing the extraordinary title of Director of the Spoken Word – briefly informing me that a scheduled repeat of the broadcast had been cancelled owing to objections which had been raised. This sort of thing, I have to confess, has quite often befallen me, though, believe it or not, in most cases I have been unaware, until it was pointed out, of the reason why. It is tempting to attribute such unawareness to a degree of innocence in oneself, or to an obsessive passion for the truth. A more likely explanation, I fear, is just a congenital awkwardness: a proneness to tread on people's toes and stumble against them, in deed and in comment. The punishment for me came – and there is always a punishment, and it is always appropriate – when, in the course of a broadcast, the producer held up a sheet of paper on which he had scrawled in large letters: 'Be controversial!'

Commander Barnes's admonition was followed by a lengthy lull in my budding career as a broadcaster, broken when I was invited to take part in *The Critics*, then young and in the spring. Incidentally, I expressed the opinion in those very early days of the programme that it could not possibly last, being too mannered, foolish, and altogether remote from the lives and interests of most listeners. Now, some two decades later, it is still going strong. When I was editor of *Punch* efforts were made to produce a parody of *The Critics* under the title of 'The Pundits', and for the purpose the scripts of past programmes were procured. Reading them through we realised that they defied parody; all we could hope to achieve would be just another *Critics* programme. The project was abandoned. This kind of thing is always liable to happen in bringing out a humorous magazine.

Being on *The Critics* involved going to a film and a play, reading a book, listening to a radio programme and visiting some sort of art show. It was one of those experiences which, though not particularly momentous in itself, yet stamps itself like stigmata upon one; the more so in my case because I have always had a rooted objection to being entertained or culturally uplifted. Having digested our pabulum, and having prepared one's own particular script – in my case, the book – one presented oneself at Broadcasting House on a Thursday in time for luncheon. Donald Boyd, an old colleague and friend of mine from *Manchester Guardian* days, presided. He has long ago retired, and I never see him, but vividly recall his brooding, ironic presence, conveying a sense – to me, most sympathetic – that human beings are always ridiculous, and never more so than when they clothe themselves in the magisterial garments of literary and artistic punditry.

Our deliberations began over luncheon (tasting, I used to reflect, of the Home Service), and received a certain amount of alcoholic stimulus. We each had an allotted role, mine being that of an ageing and already grizzled *enfant terrible*. It is the nature of mass-communications thus to require of their exponents that they should acquire and sustain a role, which in time takes over – poor Gilbert Harding for ever imprisoned in his irascibility, a Dimbleby in his pomposity, a Frost in his jocularity. We mass-communicators grow old and grey in the service of our *doppelgängers*, and may expect, like Harding, at last to succumb to them. There is no escape; if tonight I were to recite the thirteenth chapter of Corinthians on the telly, viewers would respond, according to their dispositions, by applauding or denouncing my irreverence. 'They ever must believe a lie who see with, not through, the eye,' Blake wrote. The microphone and the camera are the greatest instruments so far produced for hearing and seeing with, rather than through, ears and eyes, and have generated, in consequence, a readiness to believe lies unequalled in human history.

After lunch we went upstairs to our studio and recorded the programme. It was a talking marathon. Out of the babble of talk occasional shrill cries would emerge, like the cries of sea birds when waves are breaking on a solitary shore. I can still hear a female voice shrilly proclaiming: 'I *liked* it!' and a male one in a deeper key, but equally insistent: 'I *don't like* Raphael!' By five o'clock we were finished, and emerged into Portland Place, breathing in the air greedily after our incarceration; then, in my case, on to Charing Cross and Fleet Street and, this time, a typewriter, with a weight of dead words about my heart and a sense of a lost afternoon, if not a lost life.

A similar scene was enacted for *The Brains Trust*, in which I once or twice participated. It took place in the evening; the meal was dinner instead of luncheon, and somehow, although the food was the same, the occasion was more dignified and substantial, perhaps because, in the mass-communicators' hierarchy, Brains take precedence over

Critics. Whereas the latter only traffic in opinions, the former are expected to dispense our most sacred mystery – facts, the very sacraments of science. As a Critic I proved inadequate, as a Brain non-existent.

When *The Brains Trust* was subsequently transferred to television I was for some weeks its chairman. We performed on Sunday afternoons, after lunching together at Scott's in Piccadilly, and driving out to the fastnesses of Shepherd's Bush in a large Rolls-Royce which, as I learnt from the chauffeur, was normally used for funerals. Our set was supposed to convey a book-lined study with an open fireplace and a blazing fire. The books were mostly dummies, with a few bound volumes of sermons and Victorian poets which, for purposes of verisimilitude, could be detached; the blazing fire was electrically operated, with sham logs. On one memorable occasion John Betjeman seized one of these and waved it in the air to illustrate some point he was making about contemporary architecture.

A more popular and, to me, congenial version of the same procedure is *Any Questions?*, put out by the BBC's West Region, and, like *The Critics* and *The Archers*, a marvel of longevity. The audiences, I observe, are visibly growing older, as also, of course, are we, the performers. Shall we, perhaps, one day all drop dead to the question, put by a lady from Stroud in the studio audience, as to whether the panel would like to live for ever?

The studio audience, incidentally, on radio and television, deserves a special study by some student of politics, if not by Robert McKenzie. Watching it react, as I so often have, to instructions, in sign language or held up on a board, to laugh, applaud, groan, sob or yell, it has seemed to me a perfect image of twentieth-century universal-suffrage-democracy. One man one vote, one audience one laugh – so runs the road from Social to People's Democracy; from Locke to Lenin; from 1789 to 1984.

Television, as far as I was concerned, came like a thief in the night. I cannot pretend that I saw its great potentialities. Almost overnight one was suddenly aware of the glassy eyes of television sets staring vacantly at one across sitting-rooms, of aerials rising like dreaming spires into the city, of cameras silently closing in on one, of a microphone just too far away from one's mouth for a bite to be taken at it. Thenceforth the bulk of the citizenry were to be preoccupied, not with life itself, but with the image of life in a little screen; meeting there the great ones of the earth, watching there the contemporary scene, imagining that they have climbed in there themselves. Television has proved a great venture in collective narcissism – nature held up to a mirror instead of the other way round; all the stage a world.

It was Andrew Miller-Jones, the founding-father of *Panorama*, who first asked me to appear on television. I was to go out to Harringay where one of Billy Graham's meetings was being filmed, and afterwards to have a studio conversation with him. At Harringay for the first time I saw the cameras in operation. Subsequently, of course, I became all too familiar with that strange little procession, consisting of cameramen, sound recordist and their acolytes, all wired together as with an umbilical cord, moving concertedly, almost conspiratorially, hooded gun-microphone held aloft, their tread deliberate and restrained like a spirited horse on a snaffle. Likewise that other telly-scene – two chairs in a studio, arc-lamps overhead, cameras advancing upon one and then retreating, their little red lights glowing, making them seem bloodshot-eyed, and the floor-manager, battery at his belt, ear-phoned, raising an admonitory finger, dramatically dropped in a signal to begin.

I heard myself asking Billy Graham questions, and him answering them. It ought to have been strange, seated there together under the arc-lamps, but actually it wasn't. Everything that happens on television takes place outside oneself; there is a telly-world apart, in which one can watch and listen to oneself in complete detachment. Encounters in this telly-world might take place in outer-space for all the impression they make. I must, I suppose, have met on television at one time or another most of the eminent and the notorious figures of the day – from Bertrand Russell to Harold Wilson, from Salvador Dali to Lord Fisher of Lambeth, from Jawaharlal Nehru to Norman Mailer and six anonymous Black Muslims.

After the Billy Graham interview I appeared fairly regularly on *Panorama*. Practically everything was done live in the big studio at Lime Grove. The various items were set up, and we all assembled in our corners for transmission. Thus there might be in one corner a brass-hat with a map and a pointer ready to explain something or other, in another a bus-driver to talk about traffic congestion.

It was after I had been appearing on *Panorama* for rather more than a year that I first saw myself described, in an article in the *Sunday Express*, as a television personality – a distasteful epithet at the best of times, and in that setting abhorrent. The article featured a large blow-up of my face with the caption: 'The Face You've Got to Look at For the Next Two Years.' Up to the appearance of this article I had never been conscious of attracting undue attention as I went about my lawful occasions – at that time, editing *Punch*. Thenceforth I began to be aware of people staring at me. Did they stare because I now expected them to? Or had they been staring all along without my noticing? In any case, television *is* being stared at. One offers oneself for show, and can scarcely complain if one attracts attention, off as well as on the screen. Such fame or notoriety is peculiar to our time. In the past if someone was famous or notorious, it was for something – as a writer or an actor or a criminal; for some talent or distinction or abomination. Today one is famous for being famous. People who come up to one in the street or in public places to claim recognition nearly always say: 'I've seen you on the telly!' It is very rare indeed for them to recall anything one has said, and even when they do they more often than not get it wrong. They are the viewers, one is the viewed.

Thenceforth appearing on television was to be a part of my life. I cannot pretend that this has been a source of unmitigated satisfaction, or, for that matter, of unmitigated dissatisfaction. My feelings remain mixed. There is something, to me, intrinsically unsatisfactory about the medium, but this may well be due simply to my years. Television, on the producing side at any rate, is for the young, who have the requisite enthusiasm and energy, and who therefore dominate it. In the Television Centre I often feel, and no doubt look, like a white-haired vicar dropping in on a teenage rock-and-roll session in the church hall. The medium, as it seems to me, requires so much and yields so little. All the hours one's spent filming, in cutting-rooms, in dubbing studios; and then, hey presto! – some fleeting minutes on the screen, and all's gone for ever. I believe I never once walked off a set without a feeling of at any rate partial failure; a desolate sense that what had been achieved was miserably incommensurate with what had been envisaged.

Naturally the programmes I took to most easily were those which approximated most closely to straight journalism. Thus my part in *The Thirties* – a compilation of newsreel material of the period brilliantly assembled by Therese Denny – was really a writing job. Similarly with two other programmes we made on the rise of American and Soviet power in the twentieth century, which went out as *The Titans*, my part was, essentially, to write the commentary.

Also in the vein of journalism were television documentaries, upon which I ventured under the pleasant and stimulating auspices of Alasdair Milne. He sent me to India with Kevin Billington to recapture times I'd spent there forty years before when, as a young man fresh from Cambridge, I'd gone to Travancore (now Kerala) to teach at a Christian college. The resultant programme – *Twilight of Empire* – is the one which, of all the programmes I've been concerned in, gave me most satisfaction. Encouraged by the interest in this fragment of telly-autobiography, I had a go at a programme about my formative years, also directed with great skill by Kevin Billington – *A Socialist Childhood*.

Another documentary – this time with Jack Gold – that I much enjoyed was based on an American lecture-tour I undertook. The programme, when it appeared, was considered by some to have presented too unkind a picture of certain of the lecturing occasions and audiences, and I was criticised for having ridiculed those I was paid to address. On this basis, Swift would have been debarred from ridiculing the Anglican Church, Voltaire from ridiculing Frederick the Great, and Evelyn Waugh from ridiculing Fleet Street and press lords – which, as Euclid says, is absurd. After the lecture-tour I stayed on in America with Michael Tuchner to do the filming for a programme I'd long meditated – *The American Way of Sex*. There was, heaven knows, no shortage of material, and selecting and editing it gave, I'm afraid, a lot of trouble. Nor was the final result seen on the screen by any means satisfactory, though I impenitently take pride in it, if only because it tried to say something which, in my opinion, much needed saying: that the erotic obsessions of our western way of life are calculated to destroy love, happiness, and ultimately sex itself, not to mention sanity.

It was Grace Wyndham-Goldie who produced the idea (and who had been more productive in thinking up good ideas for television programmes than she?) for a series of programmes called *Let Me Speak*, in which I would talk with groups of young people with something emphatic to say. We began with young Jesuits, worked through young Marxists, Humanists, League of Empire Loyalists, Moral Rearmers, Anarchists and Ursuline Nuns, and ended up with John Birchites and Black Muslims. It was a strenuous, but I think rewarding, enterprise. I liked it if only because it was, by its nature, concerned with minorities, all too often ignored in these days of worship of the consensus – that false god.

Latterly especially I have found myself increasingly preoccupied with the exposition on television of religious questions. Is this even possible? I am by no means certain. If the founder of the Christian religion had been provided with broadcasting facilities, would His words have touched more hearts sooner? It does not follow. As it was, spoken to little obscure gatherings of mostly illiterate people in a remote part of the Roman Empire, they were to ring through the world for two thousand years. The waves of sound and light might have carried them further more quickly, but in the process what they gained in speed and coverage could easily have been lost in inspiration and authority. Who can tell? In any case religious programmes have been decreed, and interest in religion increases, not diminishes, with the decay of religious belief, in the same sort of way that the sick grow ever more conscious of their bodies. In a documentary about Lourdes, *Pilgrims to Lourdes*, directed by Michael Tuchner, I tried to convey something of the poignancy and miraculous cheerfulness of the sick who gathered at St Bernadette's shrine, and in another, *The Road to Canterbury*, directed by Therese Denny, to give some impression of the sort of religious questioning that is going on inside people today. The latter was open to the criticism of being too discursive and vague to arrive at any firm conclusions – apart, I should add, from the only two among those questioned who had a firm faith, a doctor and a nun. Yet it may be that this very inconclusiveness appealed to viewers who recognised in it their own case. I have noticed over the years a growing disparity between the judgements on television programmes of professional critics and experts and those of viewers. In television, as in literature and the arts, a mandarin class had been produced whose attitudes, judgements and very language diverge ever more widely from the commonalty. Another religious programme which gave me particular pleasure and satisfaction was *A Hard Bed to Lie on*, directed by Lawrence Gordon-Clark. We took the cameras inside an enclosed Cistercian Abbey at Nunraw, and produced, as I hope, a true picture of the monks and their way of life.

Now that Richard Dimbleby is dead, I suppose that I look back on a longer more or less continuous span of television appearances than any other extant performer. Nearly all of it has been under BBC auspices, though there was a period of estrangement when I fled to the bosom of Mr Sidney Bernstein, and another when, along with Ludovic Kennedy, Robert Kee and some other tellymen, an attempt was made to go into independent television production. It ended, I may add, disastrously, if not ignominiously; certainly hilariously.

My relations with the BBC have been like a marriage, with

ups and downs, infidelities on both sides, and separations, but miraculously we remain together, I suppose because, in a sort of way, we suit each other. During the years of our associations the Corporation's whole character and standards have undergone a drastic change, due, at any rate partially, to the competition of a commercial channel, and the consequent pursuit of high ratings. When John Reith shaped the BBC into a paternalistic public corporation, to be a monopoly, as far as he was concerned, for ever, he saw it as Christian in outlook, orthodoxly authoritarian in cultural matters, and, if politically neutral, as essentially as the Church of England a part of what is now called the Establishment. The structure withstood his departure for a number of years, but in time there were rumblings, and finally a break. It came in the shape of the now famous programme, *That Was the Week that Was*, directed by Ned Sherrin, which satirised in the most cheeky and usually amusing manner everything and everyone without respect of principles or persons. Thenceforth all taboos and restrictions were broken, until now, short of showing the act of fornication on the television screen (this may well come, at any rate on BBC 2), it is difficult to see what remains unsaid and undone. This process of liberation was exhilarating, though its appeal with each successive version – *Not So Much A Programme, BBC 3, The Late Show* – inevitably diminished. Satire lives by its comedy and dies by its smut; when the former is in short supply, the dosage of the latter tends to be increased, with calamitous results.

By a curious irony the BBC, famous for its propriety, began to err in matters of taste as only the respectable can when they decide to be improper, whereas ITV, which had been expected to be heinously vulgar, leant over backwards to preserve the proprieties. How strange a reversal of roles! Auntie kicking up her heels in the most indecorous manner, and Mr Lew Grade insistent that nothing should be said or done on the screen which, in the words of Mr Podsnap, would bring a blush to the cheek of a young person. How, from my point of view, even stranger that I should find myself discussing these matters before the television screen in the course of a marathon dialogue with Lord Reith himself! Yet so it happened.

The sound and video tapes and film of all these programmes will, for the most part, have long ago been very properly disposed of; the scripts remain, a high, forbidding pile, and it is from them that this volume is taken. Thumbing it gingerly over, I ask myself what, if anything, I have been communicating, and like Pilate do not wait for an answer. I even wonder whether, properly speaking, I have been a communicator at all. Readers, as I hope, will be able to judge for themselves.

Ireland
Ireland is so poor, its population is declining, they're so indolent and generally scatty, that there's no possibility of the twentieth century being set up there. And that's the place I have in mind to retire to.

An Interview with Myself

QUESTION: Mr Muggeridge, how far have you deliberately set about becoming a provocative or controversial figure with a view to attracting notice?

ANSWER: It's terrifically difficult to be completely honest in a matter of this kind. In all sorts of public presentations of oneself there's bound to be an element of showing off; something vulgar has always been recognised in being a public personage in any degree, and this is no doubt why the finest minds and the most sensitive spirits have preferred to live retired, if not monastic, existences. At the same time I think I can say with honesty that I have not sought to disagree; it's merely that ever since I began to look at the world at all, I can remember having a sort of odd view of it, as though the things that were going on, on the public stage, had nothing to do with me, and therefore seemed simply bizarre and ridiculous, subjects for ridicule. That perhaps is the source of one's reputation, such as it is, for being provocative or controversial.

QUESTION: Take, for instance, the views you've expressed about the Monarchy. Are they genuinely held or just an exercise in showing off?

ANSWER: Oh yes, the views that I've actually expressed about the Monarchy are genuinely held, but of course if you touch on a matter like that, which for a variety of reasons is a sort of raw nerve in society, what you actually say tends to get completely lost in the stirring up of public prejudice. My own genuine view is that the Monarchy is not a thing that matters very much. I think that, as it stands at present, it's a tremendous focus of absurdity, because it's an institution which is unrelated to our true circumstance. I never really said any more than that, or cared any more than that about it.

27

QUESTION: You are always denigrating people, running things down. Why are you so negative in all your attitudes?

ANSWER: What does negative mean? We've got a notion today that people must be optimistic, that people must think everything's going to turn out well. This is a very new and quite fallacious view of life. I think it is utterly ridiculous for an individual to think that through his appetites, living as a mortal man on this earth, he can be happy. Just as I think it's utterly ridiculous to imagine that any society of human beings, however well organised, however affluent the circumstances, could produce a collective happiness. If however I've taken a negative view tactically, strategically I've always assumed, and feel more than ever as I grow older, an intense optimism. In other words it seems to me that life is good, and that in some mysterious way the experience of living can only be of benefit to the individual and to all life of which he's a part. Exactly how this is, of course, one doesn't understand, but in that sense I feel completely positive in attitude, but utterly negative and impenitently negative about man's prospects in terms purely of his earthly existence.

QUESTION: Is there no one you admire?

ANSWER: Oh many people, many people, but when that question is put it nearly always means, Is there no one in power, no one famous, no one eminent, no one rich, no one distinguished whom you admire? Of course many, many human beings, the great majority of human beings with whom one is thrown into contact, are delightful people, towards whom one can feel without hypocrisy or forcing a sentiment of love. But it is true that power and the desire for power, the appetite for power and all the things that go with power, the desire to be eminent, to be admired, do bring out the basest side of human beings, and that those in authority always have been, are now, and always will be, the most despicable of human beings, and as such deserving of ridicule and non-admiration.

QUESTION: So negative, critical and pessimistic a view of contemporary circumstances would seem to make for unhappiness. Are you unhappy?

ANSWER: Not at all. On the contrary, as I get older I find myself happier and happier. Happy first of all about the earth itself which seems to me ever more beautiful each year as I watch the cycle of the seasons. About my fellow humans: those whom I know intimately and those with whom I come into casual contact seem to me ever more marvellous, so that happiness grows; but notice this is a happiness which only exists because it is unrelated to material and sensual satisfaction.

QUESTIONS: You always seem to be talking and writing about religion. Is this like a hypochondriac talking about health, because you haven't got any?

ANSWER: That depends what you mean really by religion. I certainly find that the dogmas of the religious faith to which we all belong, and on which our civilisation and way of life is based, namely the Christian religion – that these dogmas are to me completely incredible. I can't possibly and could never believe in them. But if religion means seeing that life consists of more than its phenomena, that it has a meaning which must be in transcendental terms, then I can say with perfect truth and sincerity that I am religious. I know without any shadow of doubt that the Christian religion is correct when it tells men and women that if they seek to satisfy themselves solely with what their flesh and the world offer they die in spirit. And if they want to live in the spirit, it can only be by seeing that happiness lies elsewhere than in earthly things.

Old Age
Being in my seventies I fall into a category which I understand is widely used in hospitals. They put on medical cards of people my age and over the magic letters N.T.B.R., which means 'not to be resuscitated'. I can't wait.

The How and the Why
I have always felt myself an odd man out because, contrary to the prevailing trend, I have never taken the slightest interest in the question 'How?', while being obsessively preoccupied with the question 'Why?' The various inventions of our time which have aroused so much wonder arouse none in me. Moving fast holds no thrill; the moon, as we get used to going there, will be, I am sure, no more exciting than Margate. I have no wish to have my days protracted by acquiring someone else's heart, or my perceptions enhanced by LSD or any other drug.

Contrariwise, the question 'Why?' has haunted me consistently and continuously. My earliest recollection of life is of wondering who I was, and even now I cannot sit quietly for five mintues without asking myself what is the point of my existence, if any. Compared with such questions as these, the composition of our genes or the structure of DNA seem to me of negligible interest. I should personally far prefer to have written one of Blake's couplets, or the shortest and most desultory of Tolstoy's stories, rather than have discovered penicillin or conducted a successful heart-transplant operation.

A Socialist Childhood

A fragment of autobiography

At the age of three months I was awarded a prize for being a plump baby – the only prize I ever received for anything. After this distinction my first clear memory is of my father and his cronies plotting the overthrow of the capitalist system in the drawing-room of our suburban house in South Croydon. They were, I suppose, odd conspirators – all very respectable citizens but, in my childhood eyes, men of destiny. Everything that mattered to me in those days took place in that room. There the conspirators gathered on a Saturday evening – round the fire or, when the sun was shining, by the open French windows – looking out in the garden, fortifying themselves with mild libations of Scotch and water. My mother dozed in her chair, and I did my best to efface myself, for fear of being noticed and sent to bed.

As they talked I seemed to hear a revolutionary mob, myself in the vanguard, making an assault on the Croydon Town Hall, and the sound of the tumbrils rolling along Birdhurst Gardens, as they carried the Mayor and Corporation to the guillotine. Like the early Christians waiting for the end of the world, we waited for the end of the capitalist system, which, as I confidently believed, would be largely brought about as a result of the efforts of my father and his cronies.

My father habitually left the house in the morning round about eight o'clock to go to the City, having gulped down his breakfast. I would post myself at the front garden gate to make sure of being able to accompany him to East Croydon station. As we walked along he would dilate upon the impending collapse of the capitalist system. In my mind's eye all its then citadels – banks, shops, tall factory chimneys – collapsed and fell, as though stricken in some mighty earthquake. And in their place a new, virtuous socialist Croydon arose. Not so, it would appear. This new Croydon which has arisen is neither socialist nor noticeably virtuous.

Already Croydon's office workers were rolling city-wards. Croydon East to London Bridge via Penge. It was like a bloodstream, red corpuscles swarming through the arteries of commerce, trickling into the network of little veins to nourish the muscle, the tissue, the nerves of the relentless city. My father hated his work as a ledger-clerk in a City counting house. In his eyes, he was helping to sustain the system he so longed to destroy. His real life began when the blood-stream flowed back to Croydon East, to be enriched again for the next day's course. I was waiting, anxiously on the look-out for him; with infinite relief spotted him coming up the ramp, always in the forefront – a small bearded man striding along vigorously. In those days he was everything to me; the centre of my universe.

More often than not my father went straight to the Town Hall from the station. On rare occasions I was permitted to sit in the public gallery to watch the Borough Council proceedings. The mayor presided, and spread out before him were the Aldermen and Councillors, my father among them – in those days the solitary Socialist. They seemed a majestic body, though even then a vague sense of the absurdity of authority and its trappings began to afflict me. From the public gallery I looked down enthralled, feeling myself to be in touch with the established social order itself. This was its very citadel, and my father had breached it; in him the Council had admitted to its deliberations its own destroyer. How I hung on his words when he rose to defend the virtuous trams against the villainous private enterprise buses! With what withering scorn he denounced the niggardly ratepayers' representatives whose only concern was to keep down public spending. Later my father became a Member of Parliament, but it was in Croydon rather than in Westminster that I saw him most vividly as a Socialist David pitted against the Capitalist Goliath. With his agile mind for a sling and devastating words for pebbles he would, I knew, lay them all low.

Some of my father's fellow Socialists found his patient, Fabian, municipal tactics too slow and pedestrian for their taste. They travelled further afield, bicycling – ladies daringly in bloomers, men in Norfolk suits – as far as Gloucestershire, to found a colony at Whiteway. This was to be their Arcadia. Though none of them had ever put spade to earth except to plant a geranium or bed out a lettuce, they easily saw themselves planting and reaping the golden corn they needed; providing for all their simple wants with their own toil; building their homesteads. Money, marriage and other ills were to be abolished, and happiness, based on brotherly co-operation, to prevail. Today the homesteads are in poor shape. Money, it seems, refused to be abolished, marriage reared its ugly head, brotherly love yielded to unbrotherly quarrelling. This kingdom of heaven on earth, like so many before it, failed to materialise.

Among other eccentric practices, the colonists were in the habit of bathing in the nude in a stream which ran through their land. This interesting spectacle provided me with biological instruction by the direct method. I gazed curiously at the unclothed bodies of the matrons, and with rapture at their slimmer more shapely daughters. It would surely have astonished the colonists to know, when they first came to Whiteway, that their last resting place was to be a country churchyard. After all their revolutionary purposes what a conventional and English outcome! I expect too that the then Rector would also have been astonished to know that his domain was to accommodate them throughout eternity. In life he looked askance at their sandals and their socialism, at their free unions and occasional nudity. In death they became acceptable. The English social scene has a way of absorbing everything at last – even rebellion. In any case, my education continued elsewhere.

My first school was what they then called a Board School; the local recreation ground my childhood pleasure garden, where my adolescent dreams first burgeoned. Here I first fell in love. The excitement of a school badge suddenly seen, the enchantment of fair hair falling under a round felt hat . . . and a dog-eared dictionary with her name on the fly-leaf – Dora P., Upper Fifth.

August 1914 broke everybody's recreation ground, even a schoolboy's. I was by this time at the local borough secondary school, subsequently transformed into the Selhurst Grammar School. If Waterloo was won on the playing fields of Eton, the class war was assuredly lost on the asphalt playgrounds of secondary schools like mine.

HEADMASTER: Mr Muggeridge has come to talk to you this morning, and you will know that he is an old boy of the school. Mr Muggeridge.

MUGGERIDGE (addressing the class): School in my day was a place to get away from as soon as possible and for as long as possible. Everything exciting, mysterious, adventurous, happened outside its confines, not within them. My days have not been haunted by any lingering adoration of some God-like athlete, compared with which adult fleshly love seemed coarse and obscene. Our adolescent sensuality was directed exclusively towards girls, whose persons, as we grew older, we ventured to explore in scented cinema darkness, or beside blackberry bushes in the August sun. Our South London cockney grated on the ear. Despite prefects' colours and other trappings reminiscent of Tom Brown's Schooldays we were irretrievably urchins of the suburbs. When I embarked upon the arduous but infinitely exhilarating pursuit of the meaning of things, it was from the bottom of a stony hillside, with no golden memories of lost innocence about my heart. No one ever seems to forget Eton, I easily forgot my borough Secondary School.

Cambridge is a romantic dream in the minds of those who didn't go there. It was more a realisation of my father's ambitions than of mine. To him the University symbolised all he felt he had missed in life: the magical and mysterious grace which he had seemed to see in his Fabian heroes and heroines. Now on his behalf I was to join the company of the golden youths. Always I have felt in this world something of a stranger in a strange land; but never more so than in my undergraduate days. The very air seemed heavy with tedium and boredom. The sleepy dons drained their subjects of life and interest, their falsetto facetiousness even more painful than their prosy banalities. Proletarian boys tend to succumb to Cambridge's allure. Instead of manning the barricades, they hang around in the corridors of power, join the Garrick Club, take to bathing in the morning, and dining in the evening. I found no joy in any of the University's life. It had the rank stench of a decaying class in a society which was itself in the last stages of decomposition. I took my sombre and often solitary rides to Grantchester, indifferent as to whether or not there was honey for tea, or whether the church clock had stopped at ten to three.

This sense of isolation was exaggerated by the fact that the great majority of my fellow-undergraduates had been at public schools. I did not understand their slang, play their games or share their ways. It was my first acquaintance with the upper classes and I did not like them. In my day faint derivatives of Rupert Brooke were still around, all too self-consciously unprepared for the long littleness of life, toasts of homosexual dons, pale youthful bodies, lithely swimming in Byron's pool. Already, as I saw it, the sun was setting on this golden world. It was a dream I failed to share, and, after four non-productive and undistinguished years, I gladly contracted out to spend the next six in Egypt and India. After which I became a journalist and, at the age of 26, was washed up on a desolate shore indeed – the *Manchester Guardian* in the depression.

The Industrial Revolution, leaving desolation along its trail, was now moribund. Lancashire, in the early thirties, was an outward and visible manifestation of the downfall of capitalism, as my father and his cronies had predicted in our South Croydon sitting room. I exulted to think that everything was coming to pass under my very eyes just as they had envisaged.

On the *Guardian* we worked to the famous C. P. Scott, an

old Liberal cock valiantly crowing in a neglected farmyard where weeds grew unchecked and the stench of decay rose in the air. The hopeful views we expounded on his behalf seemed to me increasingly remote from the circumstances which actually confronted us. We were looking not outwardly at the world, but inwardly at a reflection of our enlightened selves.

It had always seemed to me ever since I can remember that the only human achievement that mattered was to write. Words written and spoken were all. I envisaged many immortal works, all unwritten, and even managed to produce a few most mortal ones. I suppose when I come to die the strongest impression of life will be a sheet of white paper on a desk or in a typewriter which needs to be filled. We leader-writers were posted each in his separate perch along what was called the Corridor. Nightly we typed out our editorial exhortations – the voice of Liberalism, righteous and enlightened; putting the world to rights, telling our fellows the way that they should go, championing the downtrodden and oppressed. We believed, not entirely without reason, that our words went ringing round the world. It is so no longer. The present editor of the *Guardian* sits, not in C. P. Scott's seat, but in London. The famous *Manchester Guardian* has become the *Guardian* merely. The lights that burnt so brightly in Cross Street are growing dim. The voice is muted that spoke so confidently and so eloquently. Here in its very cradle the Liberal mind reaches its last decrepitude – becoming a civilisation's death wish.

By now I was married. Sharing my life with my wife Kitty, having our four children, has been one of those experiences that so transcends others, as well as the accompanying emotional and sensual wear and tear, that in the end there is nothing to say about it. But however she looked at it, marrying Kitty – a niece of Mrs Sidney Webb, and with other eminent social connections – was a leg-up socially. The Webbs, in relation to the hierarchy of the Left, were Ducal. From the point of view of a career – that dread word – things looked good.

In due course the Webbs, like the Whiteway Colonists, were accorded an appropriate resting place – in their case in Westminster Abbey along with the Captains and the Kings. Before this blessed consummation I, as a nephew-in-law, enjoyed their gracious favour. My father – dear man – readily stomached Mrs Webb's somewhat condescending attitude to the connection. I was not so pleased. The *Guardian*'s liberal inanities were ever more sour in my mouth. The economic depression hung over my spirits as it did over Lancashire. Increasingly Communism loomed up as the way of salvation, and Moscow as its heavenly City. I pined to be gone there. 'In Russia, Sidney and I are ikons now,' Mrs Webb said to me once, striding through Hampshire shrubland, her dog Sandy and her consort Sidney panting along beside her. By the time they came to die the Webbs were ikons here too.

It was from the Webbs' warm Fabian nest that I took off for Moscow in the autumn of 1932. They sped me on my way, clucking sympathetically. There was, as I then believed, this other paradise to go to, and thither I duly went.

Current Reflections

I don't think I've ever seen that film before. What a terrible man I was! There's a certain arrogance about myself as narrator – the way I lay down the law. I think it's rather horrible. I'd put it differently now. What is completely lacking is any humility, and I think this is not just the most important virtue, but the condition of all virtue. Compared to the written version in my autobiography, which is much more subtle and in a way faked, this is raw material – and raw it is!

But I suppose an image of oneself, however authentic, in a way isn't oneself either because the camera lies – it must do. Everybody in front of a camera, and myself in particular I regret to say, is to some degree an exhibitionist. Whereas, if you sit with a pen in your hand, you have an idea, you can alter things, try to get it exact – as far as this terrible clamorous ego in yourself will allow.

I ought to have made it clear that I was one of five children, instead of giving the impression that I was an only child. But I was undoubtedly my father's favourite, and therefore went to Cambridge whereas my brothers didn't. But I leave them out, which is pure egotism. The schoolteacher at my first elementary school, Miss Corke, knew D. H. Lawrence, who was also teaching in a Croydon school at that time. These two had some sort of affair which they both wrote about in their books. It fascinates me to think that while I was learning my multiplication tables from Miss Corke, she was learning about the dark unconscious from D. H. Lawrence at the weekends. It was probably all verbal, because he was a great talker but not such a great performer.

I'm afraid I wasn't very polite about my secondary school. It was appalling bad manners on my part. I suppose one's mind irons out the past, muffling what is disagreeable like an eternal sub-editor conforming to one's hopes and desires. But I thought that was most offensive and I wouldn't blame the headmaster if he'd intervened and said 'shut up'. He probably wrote a stiff note to the BBC.

It's curious and true, I suppose, that nobody in all history has been able to do what I'm doing now – to see themselves talking, expressing views across decades. I'm glad to have an opportunity of repudiating this figure of fifteen years ago, who to me is the most appalling S.O.B. I've seen in a long time. If you write about yourself you can say, 'Well, you misunderstood that, I didn't mean that' – but on film, there it is. It'll be interesting now to see other programmes I've made – I hope I improve!

Computers
You can leave two computers in a room by themselves without the slightest anxiety.

Judges
Most judges talk drivel the entire time.

Mini-mania
There's nothing in this world more instinctively abhorrent to me than finding myself in agreement with my fellow humans.

Keir Hardie

I've attended a great many Labour Party conferences, sitting in the reporters' gallery, and we always used to exchange a look up there when anybody got up and said 'If Keir Hardie were alive today', because we always knew we were going to hear some even greater boloney than the normal speeches. My own opinion, for what it's worth, is that if Keir Hardie were alive today he would be an eager and active member of the Right Wing of the Conservative Party.

Winter in Moscow

The England I turned my back on in 1932 was a dismal place. Old Jerusalem was falling down and no New one building. From the *Manchester Guardian* office, resounding with Liberalism's dying platitudes, I gazed disconsolately out upon the ravages of what the politicians called an economic blizzard. It seemed to me evident beyond any shadow of doubt that capitalism, as Marx had foretold, was now irretrievably moribund and doomed – offering its captive workers no hope.

So the militants among them took to the streets confidently supposing themselves to be the spearhead of a proletarian army. They – like me – fastened their eyes on the triumphant proletariat in Russia. There at least, we believed, the *Internationale* really did unite the human race. This was the Marxist paradise which I was now to report for the blameless readers of the *Manchester Guardian*. In England when the mounted police charged we shouted 'Cossacks!' Today victory might go to the Cossacks but tomorrow belonged to the workers.

This was the dream I had. Its dissolution before the harsh reality of the USSR was the pain that lay ahead. In Russia I expected to find a perfect society created by Lenin's October Revolution. What I actually found was chicanery, brutality and dictatorship.

I joined the little company of foreign journalists in Moscow, all with our due accreditations. Our impossible task was to find news when there were only handouts and lies, to report what we weren't permitted to see, and to explain what was inexplicable. In my early days there I used to spend a lot of time just walking the streets. The unending stream of people, grey-faced, anonymously clothed, had a curious attraction. Alexander Woollcott [a well-known American

41

writer and journalist connected with the *New Yorker* in its best days] told me how once, when he was standing outside his Moscow hotel, a Russian passed his hand over his fur coat and ample stomach just for the satisfaction of touching such splendour. It reminded me of living in India as a sahib in the days of the Raj.

Foreign currency – 'valuta' – was the password to the privileges we enjoyed, valid only in Torgsin shops where foreign delicacies – inconceivable luxuries – were on sale. 'Valuta' meant the sybaritic, capitalist world stumbling affluently backwards, in contrast to the penurious, Communist world striding austerely forwards. Everyone wanted 'valuta', not the bootlegged rubles we foreigners got at vastly inflated rates and carried home in newspapers like fried fish.

Those of us with families set up house – usually in dachas outside the city. My wife Kitty and I found a perch in the suburb of Kliasma. In a few select hotels facilities were even provided for capitalist style high living: *dolce valuta* within sight of the Kremlin. How ironical, I reflected, that I, a fugitive from capitalism, should for the first time in my life experience the sensation of being a plutocrat in the world's first communist state.

For us journalists, of course, there were press conferences, and we had our messages to concoct, reprocessing the processed news and submitting the result to the censors. The problem in dealing with them was, as it were, to reconcile truth with *Pravda* [*Pravda* meaning 'truth' in Russian], with truth invariably the casualty. *Dolce valuta* was the reward for keeping on good terms with them.

The big story when I arrived in Russia was the first Five-Year Plan. Stalin with the members of the Supreme Economic Council presided over the shaping and execution of the Plan like God in Genesis over the creation of the world. The Plan laid down what was to be produced, where, and how much, in every department of life from tractors to hot-water bottles. But Stalin's obsession was with heavy industry. Machines were like gods – a juggernaut requiring dedicated, unquestioning service and, above all, sacrifice. In the new Soviet theology, the turbines which continually do turn replaced cherubim and seraphim.

Soviet composers, with their symphonies of machines, provided the liturgical sacred music. The factory chimneys and glowing furnaces were the Promised Land to which Moses–Stalin was leading Marx's chosen peoples. This was the high tide of the Five-Year Plan.

At the theatre the plays we saw had names like 'Cement' and 'Slag'. Painters called their sentimental landscapes 'From a Factory Window'. Even at the Moscow Races a horse called *'Pyatiletka'* – 'Five-Year Plan' – was a dead cert. Man as producer, Man as consumer – I could hear the familiar Webbian duet intoned by Beatrice and Sidney over toast and a bright Hampshire log fire. But did this really exhaust all the possibilities? What about Man as a soul?

The ostensible hero and beneficiary of it all was the Soviet worker. Even the vast and ever-growing labour camps organised by the political police were, perversely enough, part of the cult. It was a cult of statistics to the greater glory of Stalin and his Proletariat. The newspapers were full of stories of heroic workers who pushed manganese production up to unprecedented levels. As percentages soared to ever dizzier heights, available supplies dwindled ever more abysmally.

How to relate these digits to the actual men I saw around me, borne down by the toil and deprivations of their lives. I asked for bread and you gave me a percentage. No longer 'to each according to his need'. Now only those who produced could eat. How indestructible were the Russian people, I reflected. Their mild, Slav features, their stoicism, belonged, for me, to the beloved pages of Tolstoy and Gogol – not to graphs and statistics. But this was the twentieth century, and Lenin's dictum had been 'Overtake and outstrip America' – a Wellsian vision that was later to come to pass with incalculable consequences.

Under the Plan the peasants were to provide food for the factory workers, but the produce they took to market only earned them useless rubles, for there was nothing to buy. So they humanly ate what they grew and the food queues in the cities grew longer. Stalin's characteristic response was to collectivise the farms by order and administer them by force. The peasants in turn slaughtered their cattle and ate the seed corn. With calculating callousness Stalin launched a programme of liquidation of the *kulaks* – the richer peasants – and directed the resentment of the poorer ones against them. As he made war on the peasants, the famished countryside became a place of terror. The military were called in and resistance was put down with brutal coercion. The populations of entire villages were deported, leaving them empty and deserted, as I saw for myself in the Ukraine and the Caucasus. Hundreds of thousands were herded like cattle to corrective labour camps in Siberia and the Arctic North. It was a desolating spectacle, this wanton sacrifice of millions of lives for an idea. Stalin's collective farming turned some of the richest wheatlands in Europe into a wilderness.

Through this wilderness we journalists were taken by special train to visit the Dneprostroy Dam. It was the journey I remember, not the dam. It was, I recall, a jolly affair. Someone brought along a gramophone; the railway carriage was a haven of rest and good cheer. Outside there were unspeakable horrors. 'I don't know what you're worrying about,' said the man from the Soviet Foreign Office, 'you've got plenty to drink.' We had. Most of the stations had been cleared for our passage, but occasionally there would be a little huddled group of *muzhiks*. At one station a German correspondent threw out a chicken leg he had been gnawing. The *muzhiks* hurled themselves upon it. It was one of those little quick scenes which live with one like stigmata.

'The cinema', Lenin said, 'is our greatest art,' and his followers were McLuhanites before McLuhan. The medium was the message and the message was the Party Line. The great Russian film-makers such as Eisenstein were also party hacks. As in Hollywood virtue was shown triumphing over worldliness, so in the Soviet films of the time we saw Communist virtue triumphing over bureaucratic dilatoriness.

The actualities of Soviet life depressed me more and more.

Where I had looked to find a new and better society, I found a new and better method of enslavement. The Bourbon kings claimed: '*L'état c'est moi*'. Stalin went further: '*Le peuple c'est moi*'. But the people he symbolised stood cowed in the background. It was only the élite, the *apparatchiks*, who basked in their leader's favour. To them he might be Little Father – to the rest he was Big Brother. And when he opened his mouth all the Communist dogs barked. Every thought in every mind, whatever was spoken, written, shouted, whispered – all subjected to the same centralised control. It was shattering – the more so because it gave every appearance of working. Nothing else worked – not industry, not agriculture, not the administration – but this did.

Even with Big Brother ever vigilant, things still went wrong. Why? Sabotage, of course! If weeds choked the good grain it could only be because someone had deliberately planted them. Who? Without any question traitors anxious to deprive the triumphant proletariat of their food. Likewise if production lagged it could only be because of sabotage by Russian or foreign engineers. At the great show trials the accused, many of them the Revolution's founding fathers, publicly confessed to crimes they could not possibly have committed. Their real crime was that deep inside them they had disagreed with Stalin, and their fantastical confessions, as Koestler has so brilliantly shown, were in this sense genuine. The trials, in other words, were Morality Plays, part of the mysticism of power.

In Lubyanka Prison in Moscow the GPU dealt with these class enemies, with the scapegoats of collectivisation and the Five-Year Plan. I noticed how people in the street quickened their step and dropped their voices as they passed within its shadow.

There were, however, no doubts in the minds of the tourists who were now coming to Russia in increasing numbers. For the most part they were intellectuals of the Left, Privy Councillors to be, contributors to the *New Statesman* – the flower of our Western intelligentsia. Intourist took them under its wing from the moment they disembarked at Lenin-

grad and never thereafter let them out of its sight. They
arrived in Moscow resolved to see what they had come to see
and hear what they had come to hear, their faith in the regime
and in the Intourist guides who expounded it unshakable. I
can hear them now in their eager high-pitched voices,
explaining away privations they would never have to endure
and oppression that would never reach them. 'You can't
make an omelette without cracking eggs,' Walter Duranty,
New York Times correspondent, was fond of remarking after
his umpteenth Scotch. Omelette eaters of the world unite! As
I came to grasp their almost inconceivable credulity and
naîvety, their readiness to believe anything, however absurd,
that fitted in with their preconceived notions of this Fabian
fairyland, I developed a lasting contempt for them and their
like.

Trade Union visitors were usually slightly more sceptical.
They knew that by no stretch of the imagination could
Transport House be built in Russia's green and pleasant land.
Publicly, however, they were appropriately fraternal.

The most publicised, and certainly the most fatuous, of all
the visitors to the USSR was, alas, Bernard Shaw, who came
with Lady Astor in his train:

> Hullo all you dear boobs who have been saying for a
> month past that I have gone dotty about Russia. Russia –
> her people employed to the last man and woman, her sci-
> entific agriculture doubling and trebling her harvest, her
> roaring and multiplying factories, her efficient rulers, her
> atmosphere of such hope and security as has never been
> seen before in a civilised country on earth.

Even more welcome were my aunt-by-marriage Beatrice
and her consort Sidney Webb, whose book *Soviet Communism: A New Civilisation* had been checked, they proudly told
me, page by page by the Soviet Ambassador, Mr Maisky. 'In
Russia', Aunt Bo told me one day, 'Sidney and I are regarded
as ikons.' Certainly the old ikons seemed to have had their
day.

A little church in the woods outside Moscow whose coloured walls had been surreptitiously repainted was a bright

sight in the dark woods. I remember services I went to in Russia more vividly than anywhere else. Was it perhaps because the Christian words so sweetly disparage all the things of this world, and so seemed peculiarly apt? Officially the Christian religion was due for dismantling. Unlike the State it really was to wither away, its buildings desecrated, its treasures removed and its faithful dispersed. The Father, Son and Holy Ghost had been replaced by a new and unholy trinity, Lenin, Engels and Marx. History bowed to Art, Truth to Agit Prop.

How closely, I reflected, those innumerable portraits of Lenin and Stalin resemble the Mayors and Aldermen, in leaden oils, to be seen in any Town Hall. Written history, likewise, followed, as it still does, the Party Line. Each new twist and turn of policy set the learned pens busily to work unsaying what had been said before. The sycophancy of Soviet scholarship touched depths unknown even in Oxford and Cambridge. Writers, said Stalin, were 'human engineers'. 'Book production can be planned in advance, like the production of textiles and steel.' It was sad to see old Gorky giving his blessing – I hoped a senile one – to this masquerade.

The Russians duly got their tyrant, and all the hopes that brought me to Moscow became angry dust. And so I made off with, still ringing in my ears, the insensate adulation Stalin demanded from his own captive people and was freely accorded by what passed as being the most enlightened, perceptive and humane minds of the Western world.

In February 1934, my wife's aunt, Fabian and fulsome apologist for Stalin's Russia, referred to me in her diary: 'In a little note of regret about my illness Malcolm wrote that he was "angry and bitter at the whole business of Soviet Russia". In a friendly answer I asked him why.'

'Bitter and angry, Aunt Bo, because something I believed in has turned out to be a fraud. And now there's nothing to believe in. The most encouraging thing I found in the Soviet regime was its failure. If it had succeeded, I think I should have committed suicide, because then I should have known that there were no limits to the extent to which human beings could be terrorised and enslaved. I won't send you my book, *Winter in Moscow*, because I know you'll hate it. It's an outpouring of anger and bitterness, in a way, futile.'

Looking back now, across more than three decades, I see those months I spent in the USSR in a different light. The disillusionment, such as it was, merges into a general sense that power must invariably bring out the worst in those who exercise it, and that the dream of a more humane and just and joyous collective existence, whether entertained by a St Francis or a Karl Marx or a Philadelphia Founding Father, belongs – as the psalmist puts it – to a land that is very far off.

There is also the land that is very near – I mean our earth itself and all its creatures – conveying, for those that have eyes to see, the image of another paradise at once infinitely near and infinitely distant; as Blake puts it, 'all Eternity in a grain of sand'.

Current Reflections

It was a very awkward time when I returned from Russia. First of all I quarrelled with the *Guardian* because they didn't like my coverage at all. The liberal view was that mistakes might be made but basically the regime was greatly to be admired. The general feeling was that; if you reacted strongly against a communist regime, you must therefore be equally strongly in favour of a capitalist way of life; but I didn't see any occasion to alter any judgement I'd made. Strangely enough, when I came to know George Orwell, in a sense we had this feeling in common, because he too, through his experiences in the Spanish Civil War in Catalonia, was bitterly critical of how the communists behaved there, but it didn't make him find the Franco regime any more palatable. Partisanship is expected of us all today; I had none.

An Eighth Deadly Sin

One of the peculiar sins of the twentieth century which we've developed to a very high level is the sin of credulity. It has been said that when human beings stop believing in God they believe in nothing. The truth is much worse; they believe in anything.

Russian Rumours

We foreign journalists in Moscow used to play a game of seeing how far we could go in telling Intourists tall stories about the Soviet regime without straining their credulity. I scored a big success by planting the story that Soviet citizens were so eager to devote themselves wholly to building socialism that they couldn't be induced to rest. So food shortages were arranged to ensure they should take a break, at any rate while waiting in the long queues outside food shops. My story went down very well, finding acceptance among such distinguished Intourists as the Webbs and Bernard Shaw, whose credulity would have shocked an African witch-doctor.

Is the Notion of Progress an Illusion?

A conversation with Bertrand Russell

MUGGERIDGE: My position is this – I consider that one of the major factors in reducing the world to its present rather melancholy condition has been the circumstance that human beings have been conditioned, for a variety of reasons, to believing that in some extraordinary way human life must, or can, get better and better. Now I regard this as a complete fallacy. I don't think it gets better, nor, indeed, do I think it gets worse. And I think that the only way that human beings can live sanely in this world is by recognising that, and therefore I contend that the idea of progress has been a disintegrating idea, a fundamental error, and that there's very little hope for us until it's ultimately exploded.

RUSSELL: Well, if one accepted the view that nothing that anybody can do will make the world either better or worse, one might just as well take to drink and sink into the gutter. And it seems to me that it's not the view that you really take, and you don't really believe it.

MUGGERIDGE: I must utterly disagree with that, because I don't think that not believing in progress – believing as, for instance, Christians have always believed, that human life is inherently imperfect, and that it cannot be other than imperfect, because they are imperfect – I don't believe that that has produced a sort of enervation. There's absolutely no reason why people shouldn't become richer, why they shouldn't invent things, why they shouldn't make their lives more comfortable. All that's got no bearing on the particular question that we're discussing. What we're discussing is whether human life itself is progressing, is getting finer, richer, better. In my opinion, not.

51

RUSSELL: There are, you admit, changes in our circumstances.
What you do not admit is that those changes are either for the

better or for the worse? You've maintained that they're ethically neutral, and if you hold that, honestly and sincerely, it does follow that it doesn't matter what you do at all, and that all ethical standards – all ethical and moral standards are at an end.

MUGGERIDGE: Not in the least. I'm not at all saying that changes in human life don't matter. I'm saying that they don't alter its essential character, and that if people attribute to them qualities that in fact they don't have, they are pursuing a fallacy, and ultimately wreck their lives. In other words, it may or may not be desirable that you should have things like a radio, this strange invention that is enabling us tonight to be heard by other people. It may or may not be an advantage that that exists, but it has no bearing on this idea of progress. On whether you and I are better people, more likely to understand the circumstances of our existence.

RUSSELL: I don't think one ought to confine oneself to scientific discoveries. Now, there have been savage societies in which, when a man got old, his children sold him to neighbouring cannibals, to be eaten, and I think you and I would agree that was a bad system, and we prefer the system in which old men are allowed to go on.

MUGGERIDGE: I should have said, myself, that if you added up the appalling cruelty of the time we've lived through, both collective and individual, it would create a world record, and I believe that there's some connection between that and this extraordinary illusion that human beings are progressing. Because I think that what really makes human beings humane and kind is humility, and the idea of progress is an arrogant idea. And that is probably its greatest moral disadvantage.

RUSSELL: I think that we've got to get down to a certain point. Are we thinking of better or worse only in moral terms or also in other terms. Now, if you're thinking only in moral terms, then I think there's a great deal to be said for your attitude, but I should say that a community is better, for example, in which people are healthy than one in which they are ill, although that's nothing to do with virtue.

MUGGERIDGE: Then you would look for the best human beings – for the highest human achievement in those communities which had most successfully mastered the problem of their material existence, and if you did that, you would be bitterly disappointed. I'm thinking for instance of someone like Gandhi who, though in many ways a very pig-headed man, had in my opinion a very profound idea, and his idea was that this assumption that by industrialising India, for instance, by making India richer, you would necessarily make it a better place was wrong. You may say that his whole movement was an anachronistic movement, but I think it contained a very great truth, and this is precisely the truth that I'm trying to get at in this proposition.

RUSSELL: Well, I think that that implies extraordinary limitations of human sympathy. The poverty of India was such that most children died in infancy, and if they survived they survived in conditions which were extraordinarily painful. If you had human feeling, if you had love in your heart, if you felt that you cared whether people suffered or not, you wouldn't like that; you would only like it if you put spiritual values, which you enjoy and the other fellow doesn't, above material well-being, which is very important when you get below a certain level.

MUGGERIDGE: I think that everything in the whole story of mankind which is great has come from a pursuit, however foolish and obscurantist, of spiritual values, and that everything that's base and everything that's common and everything that's cheap has come through the pursuit of material values. I want to ask you, Lord Russell, to take two human beings, extreme cases. Let's take a man like St Francis of Assisi, and let's take a man like Henry Ford. Now both these men perfectly genuinely believed that they were serving their fellows, and I consider that St Francis of Assisi's contribution to the business of human life was infinitely greater than Henry Ford's.

RUSSELL: I should deny that in toto, and I don't think you

recall what happened to the Franciscan movement as soon as he died. As soon as he died the Franciscan order turned themselves into recruiting sergeants for one of the most bloody wars in history. That was the effect that he had in the long run. Ford hasn't done anything like that. Ford was far more spiritual than St Francis of Assisi.

MUGGERIDGE: I would say that what progress really means, as I see it, is the creation of a kingdom of Heaven on earth, of perfect conditions on earth, and I believe that to be complete boloney, a complete fallacy. Whereas the other idea is the idea of human beings who can conceive a kingdom of Heaven in Heaven, a much finer, more wonderful, more productive idea than the idea of a kingdom of Heaven on earth which was Ford's idea.

RUSSELL: Where I fundamentally disagree is that I think the really important thing is that people should have compassion and sympathy – that they should mind when other people suffer. You can't be content with these spiritual values which consist of ignoring the rest of the world.

MUGGERIDGE: Of course, those spiritual values are really the only things that ever have made human beings have compassion.

RUSSELL: I should deny it – all through history I should say that people who have concentrated on spiritual values have produced hell. I think the Nazis concentrated on spiritual values.

MUGGERIDGE: Dear Lord Russell! Of all people they most believed in material values – they most believed in progress and, my goodness, what a show they created! They utterly believed it, they were tremendously progressive.

RUSSELL: If you see vast masses of populations suffering appallingly you must look for some means of diminishing their suffering.

MUGGERIDGE: Are we to understand that you don't believe in progress?

RUSSELL: You're not to understand that I foretell that there will be progress. I don't know whether there will or not. I hope there will be.

MUGGERIDGE: And what would you regard as progress?

RUSSELL: Well, I should regard it as progress if the average person was happier than he had been.

MUGGERIDGE: So would I.

RUSSELL: Now look, it's all very fine, this talk, but the majority of mankind at present are suffering from under-nourishment. Getting enough to eat is material and if you don't get enough to eat, you suffer, and I will not say that on account of spiritual values I'm content that the majority of mankind should go hungry.

MUGGERIDGE: Nor am I, nor am I. I hate the idea of any single human being being hungry; what I am interested in is how you create in our fellow men a desire that those who are hungry should be fed, and that one man should not be cruel and brutal to another; and I believe in so far that it has been done on earth, it has been done not through this idea that man can live by bread alone, but by the idea that he can't and that when you absolutely understand that he can't live by bread alone, you in fact are much more likely to give him bread than if you say he can. You see, if you are right, these immensely successful materialist societies of our day would be places of love and happiness, and in fact they're not.

RUSSELL: I didn't say they were places of love, but I do think that undoubtedly the average inhabitant of the United States is happier than the average inhabitant of India at the present day.

MUGGERIDGE: And better?

RUSSELL: There you come back to morals. I don't want to go into morals because I think morals are controversial.

MUGGERIDGE: We must be controversial, we can't divorce this from morals. It's an impossible thing to do. What I actually believe, if you want to know, is that basically there is only one thing that makes human beings seek one another's good and that is expressed in the religious concept of love;

that that alone mitigates the horror of competing and hating mankind.

RUSSELL: Now may I answer that. If you study the history of religions, you will find that they have been incredibly full of hate, of persecution, of intolerance, that they have been among the main reasons why human beings have inflicted suffering upon each other, and in proportion as religious belief has decayed, people have grown more humane.

MUGGERIDGE: I have lived in two societies where religion was systematically destroyed. One was the Third Reich, Hitler's Germany, and the other was the USSR – Russia, and in those two countries I have seen more cruelty, more callousness, than anywhere else I have ever been.

RUSSELL: That is because both of them were inculcating a new religion. They both had a religion and a new one, and new religions are more intolerant than old ones, and it was the religious intolerance that made them be so cruel and so bad.

MUGGERIDGE: I think the only thing that any human being could possibly seek to achieve is to be good.

RUSSELL: Oh good heavens, I'd cut my throat if my motive in life was to be good. I mean it seems to me the most priggish and horrible object to have in your life.

MUGGERIDGE: I think it's the only one.

RUSSELL: And if you wish to be good you're not forgetting self.

MUGGERIDGE: Of course you are.

RUSSELL: People who wish to be good are just horrible to my mind; and are completely defeating the end, they'll never be good, never, never. . .

MUGGERIDGE: It comes down ultimately to what it means to be good. Now you say this is an abhorrent idea.

RUSSELL: I said it was abhorrent to make it your motive in life to be good, which is quite a different thing.

MUGGERIDGE: But that is the very fount of Christianity.

RUSSELL: And one of my objections to Christianity.

MUGGERIDGE: You think it's a horrible religion. It's also true of every single religion that's ever been. So they're all horrible.

RUSSELL: All, yes.

MUGGERIDGE: All horrible.

RUSSELL: Yes.

MUGGERIDGE: Then you would wish that not one of them had ever existed.

RUSSELL: I should. Now look here, when the question of euthanasia was discussed in the House of Lords, a bill was brought in to legalise euthanasia, and all the noble Lords who were Christians got up and said (I paraphrase their remarks) that God sends cancer to people because He likes torturing them; and you balk Him of His pleasure if you allow them to commit suicide.

MUGGERIDGE: Well they were foolish men to say that.

RUSSELL: They were Christians, and all the Christians said that.

MUGGERIDGE: Well, I would have voted against euthanasia, because I accept the fact that life is benevolently intended; and that therefore I would never take the responsibility of saying that I, a human being, can decide to bring the life of another human being to an end.

RUSSELL: But look here –

MUGGERIDGE: Because I – I am not sufficiently arrogant to be able to say that.

RUSSELL: Look here, Muggeridge. If you say that an omnipotent creator has created this world out of benevolence, you have to go through such incredible contortions –

MUGGERIDGE: But I don't –

RUSSELL: – that you can't emerge a whole human being.

MUGGERIDGE: I can see that it's quite conceivable that there are things in life which seem to me to be abhorrent and awful, but that in relation to the totality of the experience of living, both in time and beyond time, they would be comprehensible.

RUSSELL: Let me put you the opposite hypothesis, which is just as plausible. There are, we admit, some good things in the world. The world was created by Satan, who put these good things in the world because they increased the evil of the bad things; and that would have fitted the facts just as well.

MUGGERIDGE: But I just don't happen to believe it.

RUSSELL: No, because it doesn't suit you, it's uncomfortable, no other reason except comfort.

MUGGERIDGE: Not at all, because it would in many ways be much more comfortable to take quite a different view. But everything that I've seen of life and read about life and everything I've admired in life points to the conclusion that it is in fact benevolently intended.

RUSSELL: I see. So when Giordano Bruno was burnt alive, he was tenth-rate and vulgar and the people who burnt him were great?

MUGGERIDGE: No.

RUSSELL: But that's implied in what you said.

MUGGERIDGE: It isn't at all. I think the fact that he would be burnt over a matter of belief entirely ministers to what I believe. The fact he would do it. The fact that he would think it worthwhile to be burnt, rather than assent to something which, if life were as trivial as a materialist philosophy would suggest, would have meant nothing.

RUSSELL: But why should a materialist philosophy suggest that life is trivial? It doesn't suggest any such thing.

MUGGERIDGE: It does to me.

RUSSELL: It does to you because you don't understand it.

MUGGERIDGE: Maybe that's it.

RUSSELL: I'm being very nasty, forgive me. . .

MUGGERIDGE: You're not being horrid at all.

RUSSELL: Yes I am, I'm being horrid.

MUGGERIDGE: You're not being horrid at all.

RUSSELL: I've been intolerant. . .

MUGGERIDGE: You haven't been intolerant.

Belief

I don't believe in the Resurrection of Christ, I don't believe that He was the Son of God in the Christian sense, I don't believe that He was born of a virgin. But I consider and, every day that goes by, see more clearly that what Christianity has taught, the view of life, and I don't mean any twopenny ha'penny thing like ethics, I mean a profound view of life – statements like 'if a man would save his life he must lose it', things like that – I see in them not only a profound truth, but a glowing truth, so that the perception of them is more than agreement. You could regard it as a mystical experience.

The Big Time

The ambition of the Reverend Jimmy James is to write The Times
Diary *one day. 'The Big Time' gave him the chance, and Esther
Rantzen introduced him to Malcolm Muggeridge, himself some
forty years ago a diarist on the* Evening Standard, *for some helpful
advice.*

MUGGERIDGE: I see that Lord Snooks is dead. It would be
nice to have a paragraph on that. I'd probably never heard of
him, but there would be an envelope, with 'Snooks' on it,
containing whatever mark this good man had made on society – and out of that you could fabricate. 'There will be much
sorrowing,' I'd begin probably, 'in the Army and Navy Club
today at the demise, the sad demise, of Lord Snooks, who
lunched there every day.'

RANTZEN: Didn't you go out and ask people questions?

MUGGERIDGE: No, not at all. I found it much easier to make it
up. On the whole it was more effective, because if you talked
to people – and this is one of the terrible things about television that you *have* to talk to people – the telling is excessively
boring. But if you make it up, you can make it interesting.
And then they're very pleased to open their *Evening Standard*
and find that they've said something amusing. See what I
mean?

RANTZEN: I do. So you would recommend that Jimmy should
invent something?

MUGGERIDGE: Well no, because I feel that his high moral
character incapacitates him for this job anyway. But he might
very well say, 'I am going to be an honest man'. I've known
people in journalism who do that. They nearly always finish
up as film or dramatic critics because the proprietors of
newspapers don't attach very great importance to these subjects, and it doesn't matter what you say. I think, Jimmy, just

looking at you, I could predict that if you'd gone into journalism you would have ended up as a dramatic critic.

JAMES: But do you think that I'm misguided even to want to venture into this world?

MUGGERIDGE: Well, you depress me. I think that for a man of your persuasion it shows a tendency that you should suppress rigidly.

RANTZEN: How, on Friday, should Jimmy make his column as entertaining as possible?

MUGGERIDGE: He should pretend to be outspoken, but not really be outspoken. Then you want to give the impression that you know, or are familiar with, people who are in the public eye – either through notoriety, or through something that they may have done. Celebrities.

JAMES: In a way, this is the sort of thing I wouldn't personally want to do.

MUGGERIDGE: No! This is why you don't seem to me to be shaping as a good diarist.

RANTZEN: You dislike gossip?

MUGGERIDGE: I don't. I'd rather know whom people sleep with than whom they vote for. Myself. I think it's more interesting, and more significant. I don't know whether you would agree though?

JAMES: Not really. But this isn't really the policy – certainly of *The Times* Diary – to write about such things anyway.

MUGGERIDGE: No, they've got a more sanctimonious angle, but it comes to the same thing. I think that Diary is more nauseous than most others, myself.

JAMES: I think you're cynical, Malcolm.

MUGGERIDGE: No, no, I'm not cynical, Jimmy. Cynicism means that you don't believe in anything. I think it's a great thing to be the harbinger of truth, but to relate it to things like newspapers would be really rather ridiculous. Most of the very names in the paragraphs that we've sweated over are completely forgotten. Let's see who's in today's Diary. Sir

Percy Vincent. Who knows or cares? Not I. He's likely to be the next Lord Mayor of London. You didn't know that. Now you do. Who is the present Lord Mayor, do you know?

JAMES: No.

MUGGERIDGE: Nor do I. But you'd better look him up, and do a paragraph on him. That'll test you. Find something interesting to say about the present Lord Mayor, and if you can you're going far in the profession.

Book Reviewing

I've had to review a lot of books in my life and I have to admit that I haven't always read them. What an admission! I think James Thurber put it very well when he said, 'I review a book and then, if it's a nice review, I read it'.

Journalism

One of the earliest reporters of Parliament was Dr Johnson. He wasn't allowed into the Gallery, but he used to write the speeches. And he desisted, for the interesting and, by contemporary standards, bizarre reason that he found that people were believing what he wrote. If similar scruples prevailed today in Fleet Street, it would soon empty.

Lord Beaverbrook

No other newspaper proprietor, it's safe to say, not even North-
cliffe, has stamped his product so indelibly with his own image. Yet
in the very success with which he's fashioned an instrument for
expounding and spreading his views lies the irony of his life, ostens-
ibly so successful. Rarely, if ever, has so stentorian a voice been so
little heeded. Lord Beaverbrook is by ancestry and by instinct an
evangelist. He's fought the bad fight with all his might. It's difficult
indeed to think of any cause advocated by him which has thriven. Or
of any target of the various vendettas conducted by his newspapers
who has been seriously harmed thereby. He pronounces anathema,
his mercenaries go into action, and lo, when the dust settles, the
citadel is intact, the adversary unhurt.

Twilight of Empire
India revisited

When I was twenty, the world seemed a place to explore. Subsequently, God knows my ageing carcase has been hauled about this earth's surface often enough. Even so, that first occasion, waving goodbye to everyone and everything I knew, and making off, remains unforgettable. On a cold, misty December day in the year 1924 I sailed for India.

After forty years I returned there. In the intervening time the world has changed out of all recognition – and I with it. Yet at first glance there seemed no difference in the people and the scene which so long ago had so enchantingly contrasted with the south London suburb where I lived with my family; and Cambridge where I'd spent four unprofitable years. It was an embodiment of all I'd ever imagined about the tropics and the Orient. The same backwaters, the same boats and boatmen. Of course, I was young when I first came and, I suppose, innocent. Everything was new and fresh. Was it really as smiling a place as it had seemed in my memory? Travel, I know, narrows the mind, and the passing years dull the judgement. Even so I was still enchanted.

As an undergraduate I'd agreed, as a result of a casual encounter with a missionary, to teach at a Christian college at Alwaye in what was then Travancore and is now Kerala in the southern tip of India. The terms of employment were indeterminate. I had only the vaguest notion of where Alwaye was, and I was by no means particularly a Christian. In those far off days we tried to convey our contempt for the world and its ways by despising success, and cultivating improvidence – a bizarre sort of romanticism I suppose. But I had no thought of embarking on a career: it was going somewhere, anywhere; and doing something, anything.

But, of course, one forgets. On that first journey there

must have been many places along the way: a great variety of impressions. The one that sticks in my mind is arriving at Alleppey. So many brown faces and bodies crowding round and, as it seemed, shouting at me. And I, a white man, a sahib, in a suit and a topee. I remember the feeling I had of panic and even terror – the sense of isolation. At the college it was, of course, different. But I couldn't but wonder how I was going to be received this time, returning after so long an interval – a stranger.

MUGGERIDGE: It's marvellous to be back. . . . The river – you go straight down there to the river, don't you?

INDIAN: That's right. Straight down.

MUGGERIDGE: I think I shall go and bathe. The river seems to have maintained itself through the years?

INDIAN: The one thing they didn't change.

MUGGERIDGE: Yes – no change in the river.

There's plenty of change in me though. I used to swim across and back so easily, but not now. Half-way was quite enough, and even that partly perhaps to show off. It's extraordinary how large a part this river played in my life at Alwaye. Besides bathing in it I had a little boat of my own to paddle along. Whenever I've thought of Alwaye, it's the river I've seen in my mind's eye. Well, now I've seen it again with my other eye.

What a joy to find old colleagues and students; so many of them. Familiar faces though, like mine, grown old.

INDIAN: I remember one very interesting incident when you were teaching here – I was a student then. You had a contempt for annotation –

MUGGERIDGE: Yes, correct!

INDIAN: And one Indian professor, a Brahmin gentleman, visited the college – he was author of so many annotations. He visited the college, and he gave a lecture on Shakespeare; and you presided over that meeting. And in your presidential remarks you said something like this: 'If I go to heaven, which I very much doubt, I shall ask of God one favour. And that is to send Shakespeare down to earth again, and make him sit a Madras University examination in Shakespeare, just for the fun of seeing him fail.'

MUGGERIDGE: Well, I'm sure Shakespeare would fail.

INDIAN: Yes, I'm sure too.

MUGGERIDGE: The question is: whether God would pass an examination in theology? What do you think about that? It's an awkward question.

I've never been such a regular letter-writer as I was at Alwaye: long ones home every week, meticulously describing my life, thoughts and emotions. With preposterous conceit I asked my father to keep them for posterity. He did keep them, but only for me, not for posterity. In one, soon after my arrival, I described a typical Alwaye day. 'I get up at five-thirty – no staying-in-bed problem. As soon as one wakes one's only desire is to bathe, normally in the river. Then at six-thirty my servant, Kuruvilla, brings me tea and bananas. I read for a while – lately Whitman and Tagore. From seven to nine I prepare lectures; and between nine-thirty and one I teach. In the afternoon I sleep till three; read from three to five, and then take exercise – either tennis or a walk, followed by another swim in the river. It's a sort of monastic existence, but I quite like it. My servant's a good soul, but a perfect fool. Once I was smoking on my bed and a box of matches went off and burnt my hand. I shouted to Kuruvilla for ointment. He brought me first Brasso and then toothpaste. On another occasion he used communion wine to light the primus.'

Education, the great mumbo-jumbo of the age, was as avidly in demand in India as elsewhere. It's conducted in a foreign language – English, and related to an alien culture. Little Indian boys used to be taught the names and dates of the kings and queens of England; sometimes even the promontories round our coast. Our Alwaye classrooms had no sides to them. Holding forth one could see the green paddy-fields and the brown shining bodies of the men and women working in them. Their weird, echoing songs broke into counterfeit words like the sound of the sea in a dark cave. Senior students, such as mine, ploughed through the Elizabethan dramatists and the Lake poets. 'Dryden,' I would proclaim, having culled the phrase from some outline or short history of English literature, 'found English brick and left it marble.'

Education was about the worst thing we did to India; and, appropriately enough, contributed to our departure. Wasn't it predominantly enraged and unemployed graduates who chased us out, hurling after us curses and copies of the *Oxford Book of English Verse*?

Teaching always bored me as much as being taught, and I escaped with relief whenever possible from the classroom. On 19 April 1925 I wrote to my parents: 'One of the pleasantest things about living here is to go by boat through the backwaters, not a motor boat – but one of the primitive ancient ones, propelled along by boatmen. You stretch out under a wicker shelter; fall asleep to the boat's rhythm; then wake up to find everything bathed in moonlight, with boatmen singing a kind of chant as, leaning on their poles, they walk up and down the whole length of the boat.'

I belonged to the generation that was still wild about nature. We looked at sunsets and sunrises with appropriate rapture; we tramped about the countryside; we sought out remote eminences; we paced along moonlit beaches. We even read Wordsworth. To one so conditioned this Travancore countryside was a sort of ecstasy. At all times and in all seasons glowing with luxuriance. I thought when I first saw it – and I think still – that it's one of the most beautiful places in the whole wide world.

Living as I did almost exclusively among Indians, wearing Indian dress, eating Indian food, I had little contact with the Raj and its sahibs. Travancore was an Indian state, ruled over by a maharajah. This was Indian India. The all-powerful

Government seemed very far away. Its representative was the British Resident, Cotton, who, tired perhaps of the local sahibs, occasionally invited me, a non-sahib, to visit him. 'Cotton', I wrote home, 'is the focus here of all snobbishness as far as the local English community are concerned. An invitation from him is equivalent to one from the Palace. When he drives to the capital, Trivandrum, the river ferries are held up in case he should be delayed even for a few minutes. Indians fall over themselves to get into his good graces. His house, Bolghatty, is like a south-sea island, with palm trees, and a breeze always blowing. I quite expected to see darkies and hear banjoes playing. Instead there was an Indian brass band, somewhat mournfully and tunelessly grinding out "Sussex by the Sea". Cotton was waiting for me at the jetty: a solid man, well turned out, wearing stays I should suppose; everything in perfect order. Ice in the drinks – a great rarity in these parts; two not so young ladies, elegantly dressed; and some sort of visiting newspaper-owner with a small goatee beard, who dilated upon how everywhere he'd found the "natives" loyal. There's something false, decayed, hopeless, about the whole English way of life in India.'

After two years at Alwaye I had become ill; and leaving India was a relief – something I'd looked forward to and even longed for. The heat and dust and hopelessness had become oppressive. Yet mixed with a sense of relief was a kind of regret which remained with me. One may discount the old bromide about India's spirituality, and still realise that in some mysterious way eternity looms larger on these shores than elsewhere. In Alwaye I thought I caught a glimpse of eternity which, I am thankful to say, through subsequent vicissitudes and follies has never been totally eclipsed.

It was ten years before I again saw India, and then it was a different me and a different India – Calcutta, surely one of the ugliest and most squalid cities in the world. Created by the English on a swamp, its warm, humid air suggests a swamp still. I had become a journalist – a dubious trade. My part was

to sit at a typewriter, tapping out portentous editorial pronouncements. 'It is to be hoped that these two great peoples,
the English and the Indians, whose destinies etc. etc., history
has etc. etc., will find it possible etc. etc., to the enrichment
of both their etc. etc.' – what rot!

Newsprint like ourselves is mortal, and in a matter of
decades moulders away. Perhaps fortunately. Dust to dust.
Oh printed word, where is thy sting? It takes a wise editorialist to recognise his own editorials. Browsing about among
the editorial columns of these papers, I ask myself which of
them I wrote. Did I for instance write, 'If the disarmament
discussions have produced as their only obvious consequence
the determination in some countries to seek peace through
the argument of increased equipment for war, this itself by its
bitter incongruity is forcing statesmen here and there to seek
means of renewing the discussions for some wider aim'?
Honesty compels me to admit that I might have.

The main preoccupation of Indian newspapers during this
period was of course the question of independence or *swaraj*.
Now I see that on 22 November 1934 there was an enormous
news story with a heading right across the main news page, a
most unusual thing, referring to the report of the Joint Select
Parliamentary Committee in Westminster on Indian con-
stitutional reform. And the editorialist, perhaps me,
describes this 'as a State paper of the highest historical importance, whose language is adequate to the gravity of the
scene'. Neatly put. But who today remembers or cares anything about this State paper of the highest historical importance? Grave the scene may have been, but it was clearly
irrelevant to anything that had, could or would happen, in
India or elsewhere.

Today, of course, the Calcutta *Statesman* is a rather different paper; 'home' is no longer England but India. It still has
plenty of Joint Parliamentary Committees, but they're
domestically produced. And there are no knighthoods any
more in Bengal.

'Let this monument erected by the voluntary donations of

thousands and thousands of his subjects throughout his Indian Empire, the rich giving of their wealth, and the poor of their poverty, bear witness to their grateful memory of his virtues and his might. He was the father of his people. His sceptre ruled one fifth of the dwellers on earth, his reign was a blessing to his well-beloved India, an example to the great and an encouragement to the humble. And his name shall be handed down from father to son throughout all ages, as a mighty emperor, a merciful ruler, and a great Englishman.'

That inscription was written, presumably without a smile, in 1911, the year of the Great Durbar, and related to King Edward VII. It indicates the mood of confidence which animated the British rulers of India so shortly before, as it turned out, their final departure. It was in such a mood that they set about constructing what they thought was going to be their own enduring capital, New Delhi, whose walls were rising in my time.

On seeing the plans of New Delhi, Clemenceau is said to have remarked that it would make an even finer ruin than the six or seven other ruined capitals in the vicinity. So far, the walls still stand, though the British have gone taking their Viceroy with them. There are no ruling princes to sit in the chamber designed for them. A bewigged Mr Speaker presides over the Lok Sabha, where honourable and right honourable members debate in accordance with the Westminster rules. In addition to the *Oxford Book of English Verse*, we gave India the Ballot Box. Likewise an inappropriate gift and already second- if not third-hand when presented.

Journalists have to follow governments as sharks swim in the wake of big liners. I followed the governments to Simla, one of the sharks to whom occasionally officials would throw a morsel of news. It was my business to convey, explain and expound to the Viceroy's distant subjects the policies and purposes of his government, if any. Who, I wondered, would be occupying Viceregal Lodge now that there was no Viceroy? Who the Commander-in-Chief's house, and all those official residences carefully graded by the Office of Works so that one could tell at a glance the status or salary of the occupant? Simla without a Viceroy – inconceivable! What astonishing if not crazy arrogance for the alien government of a sub-continent to transfer itself to this mountain eyrie just because some of its top personnel found the heat oppressive in the plains below. As though England should be ruled in the summer months from the Dolomites, with Whitehall and all the requisite clerks and files transferred there accordingly.

Simla at least we English created. It is our Taj Mahal. Royal Tunbridge Wells in the shadow of the Himalayas – Cheltenham on the world's roof – as English as marmalade. There is even a bandstand where on Saturday evenings a military band used to play selections from Gilbert and Sullivan and Colonel Bogey, The British Grenadiers, echoing away towards Tibet. Nothing anywhere to suggest it was India, except, of course, Indians.

With the Raj over and the government gone, I think I half expected to find Simla deserted. Not so. Offices and residences all occupied, typewriters tapping away as merrily as ever, files circulating, peons dozing, brown burrasahibs borne to and fro in rickshaws as white ones once had been. The white sahib has been dethroned, but his spirit goes marching on. In the Gaiety Theatre amateur theatricals still being rehearsed, but in Indian English.

'Then, old chap, it is this, I love your wife.'

'Oh that.'

'What do you say, old boy?'

'You're a bounder, sir. I've a good mind to give you a sound thrashing.'

'What a lot of twit. Are you going, old chap?'

'I bloody am – damn everything.'

How strange it would have seemed to Gandhi – he who recommended salvation through the spinning wheel and home-spun, all the ancient Indian ways!

It was a strange sensation to saunter up the winding empty drive to the Viceregal Lodge – no sentries now, no attentive

'In Russia, Sidney and I are regarded as ikons.' Beatrice and Sidney Webb travelling to Leningrad, 1932.

Malcolm Muggeridge in 1925 at Alwaye.

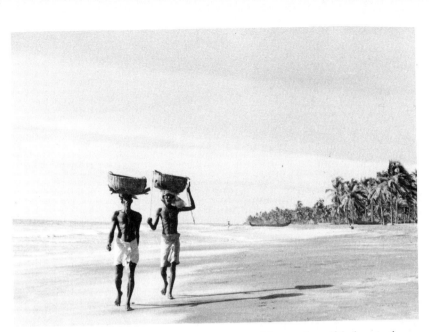

Tranvancore, now Kerala, 'a sort of ecstasy . . . one of the most beautiful places in the whole wide world'.

Viceregal Lodge, Simla, 'no sentries now, no attentive ADC's'.

With Amrita Shergil. 'She was gay, alive, beautiful; a combination of qualities not unduly plentiful in Simla, or for that matter anywhere.'

ADC's. Those gilt-edged invitation cards, once so thankfully received, so triumphantly waved in the faces of the bearded Sikh bodyguard. 'His Excellency requests the pleasure. . . .' His Excellency did not request in vain.

And now, shutting one's eyes outside the main entrance, one can imagine everything as it was before. Those garden parties: the guest list extending down to clergymen and even missionaries, to the humbler grades of Indian officials with their wives in coloured saris. The Viceroy – Lord Willingdon in my time – in grey frock-coat and matching top hat, a slight stooping figure, the Vicereine ebullient in mauve, with a sunshade, smiling to left and right that toothy unrecognising smile of great personages. The gardens and the lawns remain, but the people have gone. No more garden parties ever, I should suppose, in this place. Inside, it's like a stage being dismantled when a play's run is over. The lights are out, players and audience have dispersed. These sometime corridors of power are empty and deserted, they are rolling up the carpets in Viceregal Lodge, and we shan't see them spread out again in our time.

How extraordinary to have been the Viceroy, living in this country house among these mountains, with, below, the teeming plains of India where a fifth of the human race live and die, he their absolute ruler, responsible not to them, but to a parliament thousands of miles away, under grey skies and by a grey river in England. I saw an empire ruled from here, and have lived to see that empire and all its trappings disappear as though they'd never been. Now they're largely forgotten, and only linger on in minds like mine with their own bizarre reasons for remembering.

Here we, the guests invited to dinner, lined up, the ladies smoothing down their dresses in preparation for the curtsies into which they were shortly going to plunge, the gentlemen making sure that all their orders and decorations were correctly placed, that their fly buttons were fastened and that their braces weren't showing. Then the band begins to play, and there's a shout. Their Excellencies! And in they come, the frail Viceroy bent more than ever with the weight of hardware that's fastened about his person. The Vicereine still in mauve, this time an evening dress with a red sash across it and a coronet on her head. They pass along the line of guests, a friendly word for everyone, an ADC at their elbow to make sure that they don't forget a name. And there, far away at the end of the line, is Muggeridge Sahib in a tail coat, no decorations, no orders, but very conscious of the three chota pegs he had before leaving to keep up his spirits; holding his own, just. Then when all this rigmarole at last is over, in we joyously go to dinner.

How extraordinary it is to find the most important prop of all still miraculously in its place in the middle of all this debris – the Viceroy's throne, with the silver footstool in front of it. I must say I never thought I should ever sit in it. The Vicereine on her throne on one side of him and the Governor of the Punjab on the other. And before him milling about, rajahs and maharajas, hopeful of some extra gun salutes, officers hopeful of promotion, officials dreaming of honours to come – CBE's, Stars of India, perhaps the Bath itself. The Viceroy was in a position to satisfy them all. Seated on his throne he was the repository of power and the fount of patronage. Let's see how he struck me at the time. In my diary there's an entry: 6 May 1935 'At Viceregal Lodge yesterday, spoke first with the Vicereine, Lady Willingdon, a noisy, energetic atrocious woman, yet not without a certain vulgar fascination. At this point an ADC hove in sight, to take me away and over to the Viceroy. Somewhat unusual to be moved straight from her square to his. I was duly flattered. Willingdon was tremendously like an old beau in a Restoration comedy. With unusual animation he began by saying (and one almost expected him to take a pinch of snuff and flick his handkerchief), "You know people say this country's difficult to govern, actually it's not, you know. I find it perfectly easy to get on with these fellows. I've found it the easiest country in the world to govern." In all the circumstances a pretty extraordinary statement, but I let it pass. "I believe in Providence," he went on. "But for that I'd never have been able to carry on." A grey old fellow, full of egotism, but with a kind of charm, not in the least pompous, absolute ruler over some hundreds of millions of Indians, and a believer in Providence.' Alas, poor Viceroy, yet why 'alas'? The end of power is always more exhilarating than its beginning. I much prefer Napoleon on St Helena to Napoleon being crowned by the Pope in Notre Dame, Hitler in his tank-tangled bunker to the sieg-heils of Nuremberg. In the days of its functioning, I used to hate this popinjay court up here. Its disappearance into furniture vans is one court the less. Let the bell which summoned the Viceroy's guests to dinner toll for it now.

No one, apart from a few power maniacs and fools, allows public affairs to take precedence over private ones. Thus I'm delighted to note in my Simla diaries that my own personal affairs loomed much larger than the news I was supposed to be covering. King George V's Jubilee, which must have been a tremendous affair, seems to have passed me by. For one bare mention of the King George V Jubilee there are pages and pages about becoming acquainted with Amrita Shergil, now generally recognised as the outstanding modern Indian painter – then of course largely unknown. She's dead and I'm old, and our brief but intense intimacy mattered to no one. A portrait of me by Amrita now hangs in the National Gallery of Modern Art in Delhi, in a room dedicated to her work. She was gay, alive, beautiful – a combination of qualities not unduly plentiful in Simla, or for that matter anywhere. She studied at the École des Beaux Arts in Paris and sometimes, rather affectedly I'm afraid, we'd speak French together. I remember how when she came to see me off, at the station at Simla when I went away, she said there'd been some *beaux moments*'. I agreed, and I never saw her again.

Cemeteries are likely to be the most enduring of all the British Raj's memorials. I find the graves that we left behind us more poignant and more eloquent than other traces of our short occupancy of India. Cemeteries lashed by monsoon rains, baked by ferocious suns, under so alien skies. Or up here in Simla, on a quiet hillside. Many of the sahibs died young. Mortality was high among them in the early days.

Whatever brought them to India in the first place – cupidity, restlessness, ambition, missionary zeal, or just chance – they served the country and its people according to their lights. I never liked them, they were not my sort of person – for the most part self-satisfied and self-important, and at all levels, from the private soldiers to the Viceroy, corrupted, as it seemed to me, by the excessive subservience of their Indian underlings. Yet those whose mortal remains here in Simla, and elsewhere, will abide in India for ever need not be abashed among the ghosts of other conquerors. They were few, some ten thousand. And they kept four hundred million Indians in approximate order and security and, by the abysmal standards of this land, fed. On the last page of my Simla diary I wrote the words 'Twilight of Empire'. I never saw the morning or the noontide. Only the twilight. Nor did I stay to see night fall, but made off elsewhere.

Nationalism
The division of the world into sovereign nationalist states is an outmoded thing. We may not live to see the end of it but it's going.

Education
In our society, the belief that the road to Paradise is paved with A levels is held at least as tenaciously as any article of Christian dogma in the days of Torquemada.

The Death of Nehru

I was in Travancore when Nehru died. It was quite extraordinary. We were driving along and didn't know, and we suddenly saw these processions that were forming spontaneously; they just formed into processions going nowhere. Everyone was completely silent and you heard this pat-pat-pat of feet, bare feet on the dusty roads, and that is all you heard. Nehru was in a way the last Viceroy. Now he was dead and that was the end of it.

Let Me Speak

Empire Loyalists endeavour to explain themselves

MUGGERIDGE: One may wonder how, since the British Empire patently no longer exists, it's possible to be loyal to it. Can one be loyal to a defunct Empire, or have perhaps these young Loyalists transferred their allegiance to the British Commonwealth. Is it now Mr Jomo Kenyatta, Dr Nkrumah and Dr Banda, who fire their blood? Somehow, I doubt it. But let's see.

MALE LOYALIST: We see no reason to change our prior title because of the aberrations of successive socialist and conservative administrators.

MUGGERIDGE: I don't think you quite understood my question. Can one be loyal to something which is no longer in existence?

MALE LOYALIST: The British Empire still exists. It may be not under its former title, but a spirit of unity still remains between the British nations. I mean Canada, Australia, New Zealand, and indeed Southern Rhodesia.

MUGGERIDGE: But you see, when you for instance say that the Conservatives and the Labour party have equally betrayed this Empire, I don't think you'd find many people in Canada or Australia to agree with you.

FEMALE LOYALIST: They perhaps disapprove of our methods or some of the things, but on the whole they feel that they are being sold out by white politicians; and this is what we feel too.

MUGGERIDGE: Isn't it curious that they return governments by the ordinary operation of Parliamentary democracy which participate in these processes of what you call 'betraying the heritage of the white man'? Isn't that curious, or do you think that democracy itself is a fraud?

FEMALE LOYALIST: I think democracy is impossible.

MUGGERIDGE: But then what sort of government do you want to have?

FEMALE LOYALIST: I think a monarchy is a fine thing, it's a fine institution, about the safest one you can ever achieve.

MUGGERIDGE: But you mean a monarchy in which the monarch exercises power?

FEMALE LOYALIST: Yes, a monarchy, when the queen is not the figurehead of politicians who use her as a tool, but when the queen or the king has real power.

MUGGERIDGE: Then what you would like really would be for the Queen to rule us?

FEMALE LOYALIST: Yes to *rule* us, not to be a puppet.

MALE LOYALIST: We have no opinions as a League about the internal political structure of our country. We are concerned with the fall from grace of Great Britain; her decline from greatness.

MUGGERIDGE: Yes, but would you say that was entirely due to politicians, or do you think perhaps two world wars have been a factor in producing that result?

MALE LOYALIST: Mainly due to the lack of spirit of governments acting under duress from the American government.

MUGGERIDGE: Do you mean that, if we had not been subservient to America, we would today, despite two world wars, despite nuclear weapons, all those things, exercise as much power in the world as we ever did?

MALE LOYALIST: We wouldn't be the football of fate, as we are at the moment.

MUGGERIDGE: But those are phrases, my boy, they are phrases. The point is there's such a thing as power, and power is represented by wealth and weapons.

MALE LOYALIST: That's precisely why we want to maintain our links with British people throughout the world. So there's no question of our standing alone.

MUGGERIDGE: But look at facts today, as they are. There are ten million, eleven million Australians far away in the Antipodes, on the fringe of an enormous continent, with a thousand million Asians round them.

FEMALE LOYALIST: I bitterly resent the implication they should welcome Asian immigration –

MALE LOYALIST: Yes, indeed –

MUGGERIDGE: All right – bitterly resent it – possibly reckessly – but bitterly resent it. Now, how if there is an atomic war are those people going to be defended? Do you imagine there's anything that we could produce here that would enable us to defend them?

MALE LOYALIST: We've got the V-bombers, what do you think they are for?

MUGGERIDGE: Do you want to break the American alliance?

FEMALE LOYALIST: Yes, yes.

MALE LOYALIST: No – no.

MUGGERIDGE: There you are.

MALE LOYALIST: Mr Muggeridge, it so happens that at this very moment Indonesians are being trained in the United States to attack Malaysia.

MUGGERIDGE: Come on, tell us how you know that?

MALE LOYALIST: It's been reported in *Human Events*.

MUGGERIDGE: A magazine that I happen to know.

MALE LOYALIST: If you took the trouble to read it you'd learn a great deal from it –

MUGGERIDGE: Well now, let's move on. What about your methods, what about the methods that you employ in order to promote your ideas? I was the recipient of some of the attentions of your organisation at one time.

MALE LOYALIST: In which case you probably know how effective our methods are?

MUGGERIDGE: Yes I do. You came down to my house, or at

least some of you did –

MALE LOYALIST: We don't want to hear this story –

MUGGERIDGE: I just wondered what you hoped to achieve by doing things like that, that's all.

MALE LOYALIST: Well it seems to have worried you.

MUGGERIDGE: Not at all, I was glad to have the opportunity of making the acquaintance of some of you.

MALE LOYALIST: We, Mr Muggeridge, reserve the right to bring our case before the public by making peaceful demonstrations.

MUGGERIDGE: What do you call a peaceful demonstration?

FEMALE LOYALIST: We have never once offered violence. No, we have once offered violence, when an old man slapped a much younger man than yourself in the face for insulting the monarchy.

MALE LOYALIST: As indeed you did, Mr Muggeridge, if you remember, in a foreign magazine.

MUGGERIDGE: I expressed in a magazine –

FEMALE LOYALIST: Cheap personal remarks –

MUGGERIDGE: Certain ideas that I had –

FEMALE LOYALIST: Cheap personal remarks –

MUGGERIDGE: Now you don't of course know what's meant by freedom, but that's what freedom means.

FEMALE LOYALIST: But, Mr Muggeridge, we don't insult people that by virtue of their position cannot hit back, such as the Queen.

MUGGERIDGE: The monarchy is a public office.

MALE LOYALIST: Not the monarchy, Mr Muggeridge, but the Queen –

MUGGERIDGE: I was talking about the monarchy, and the monarchy is a public office, and as a public office every free citizen is fully entitled to express his opinions about it. If you don't understand that, then you don't understand what a free society is. And if you think that by shouting and scrawling things on people's houses and so on you're making a point, that's where you're mistaken. There's only one way to make a point, and that is by argument.

MALE LOYALIST: A dirty cheap article.

MUGGERIDGE: That's your opinion, that's your opinion –

MALE LOYALIST: It's a general opinion –

MUGGERIDGE: I simply say that as a free citizen of a free country I enjoy the right to express what opinions I hold about anything. And if people like you ever get into power, this is precisely what would come to an end.

FEMALE LOYALIST: But we say nothing but the truth, Mr Muggeridge.

MUGGERIDGE: Well, I think the way you behave –

MALE LOYALIST: We behave!

MUGGERIDGE: – suggests to me that your sympathies lie with people who have used violence to express –

MALE LOYALIST: Such as whom?

MUGGERIDGE: Such as Fascists.

MALE LOYALIST: Well-known smear, we might have expected that –

MUGGERIDGE: You have no sympathy with them?

FEMALE LOYALIST: None . . .

MUGGERIDGE: Nor their leaders?

MALE LOYALIST: No – none whatsoever.

MUGGERIDGE: Are you racialists?

MALE LOYALIST: What do you mean by that?

MUGGERIDGE: What I mean by racialism is the insistence on the superior rights of one race over another, as is happening for instance in South Africa. Three million people saying that for all eternity we must be dominant over ten million people. That's racialism. Do you agree with that?

MALE LOYALIST: It is simply the maintenance of a civilised government as opposed to the Congo.

MUGGERIDGE: So that you are saying that it is right that three million people must for all time –

MALE LOYALIST: It's unavoidable, there's no question of right or wrong –

MUGGERIDGE: I take the position that it is inconceivable historically that three million people should for ever hold dominance over ten million.

MALE LOYALIST: What about what is happening to the white people in Kenya and Ghana and other parts of Africa, and Belgian women in the Congo. Is that what you would like?

FEMALE LOYALIST: I suppose you would agree that the white people had no right to suppress Mau Mau, because Mau Mau was the majority opinion.

MUGGERIDGE: I didn't say that white people had no right to suppress Mau Mau – I haven't even said what my views on South Africa are.

MALE LOYALIST: Mr Muggeridge, do you defend the tyranny in Ghana? Do you defend the harsh laws?

MUGGERIDGE: I don't defend, my boy, I –

MALE LOYALIST: This programme is called 'Let Me Speak'. Why don't you let me speak?

MUGGERIDGE: I'd be delighted. I want to hear you –

MALE LOYALIST: I'm asking you a string of questions.

MUGGERIDGE: Right – ask your questions.

MALE LOYALIST: Do you agree with –

MUGGERIDGE: Ask me a question and I'll answer it.

MALE LOYALIST: D'you – why don't you let me get it out first.

MUGGERIDGE: Come on –

MALE LOYALIST: I'm trying my best.

MUGGERIDGE: Come on then – get it out.

MALE LOYALIST: Do you agree with the present policies of the government in Ghana which has suppressed liberty?

MUGGERIDGE: I don't agree with the suppression of liberty anywhere or in any circumstances, in any community, and in so far as I have tried to pursue one idea throughout my life, it is that, to *hate* it wherever I find it. And whenever I find a group of young people like you, for whatever motives, being attracted by this idea of a few dominating many, because they are going to give them order and good government, I watch out.

MALE LOYALIST: Do you also attack the way Communist Russia has enslaved twelve great nations and about 84 million people?

MUGGERIDGE: If you took the trouble to look up newspaper cuttings and things that I've written, you'd find that there was probably nobody who had protested longer or more consistently against such things as that.

MALE LOYALIST: It's easy for you to speak, Mr Muggeridge, because if violence did come to South Africa you wouldn't suffer one iota, would you?

MUGGERIDGE: Nor did I suffer when the Hungarian Revolution took place, nor have I suffered in a great many cases in which violence has been done to a principle in which I believe. But that doesn't prevent me from protesting against them.

MALE LOYALIST: You're not going to suffer if stability and order and law does break down in South Africa, or anywhere else.

MUGGERIDGE: You have just characteristically made exactly the same point again.

MALE LOYALIST: You didn't understand it the first time.

MUGGERIDGE: I understand it perfectly! If you are saying that no man may uphold a principle unless he is directly involved in the consequences, then you would deny the right of people through the centuries to express their views about principles.

MALE LOYALIST: I'm not –

MUGGERIDGE: You are –

MALE LOYALIST: I'm simply questioning your judgement. But can we get back to Dr Nkrumah and Kenyatta, and various other –

MUGGERIDGE: I asked whether your loyalty to the Empire extended to the Commonwealth.

FEMALE LOYALIST: Our loyalty extends to the white people.

MUGGERIDGE: Not to the modern Commonwealth?

MALE LOYALIST: We accuse this government of treason in betraying the white people in Kenya to Kenyatta who is the manager of Mau Mau. You might remember that.

MUGGERIDGE: Now what would you have done about giving Kenya its independence, what would you have done about that?

MALE LOYALIST: Kenya is not ready for independence, and it never will be. I believe the white people have to rule.

MUGGERIDGE: And you think empires are desirable –

MALE LOYALIST: This one was in its time, and this one was betrayed before its time ended.

MUGGERIDGE: The ends of empires are chaos, they always have been.

MALE LOYALIST: There are bigger barbarians leading black Africa than there are in South Africa or Southern Rhodesia.

MUGGERIDGE: This might even be true, this might even be true.

MALE LOYALIST: Well, why do you want to subject these people to a tyranny of their own kind – black over black?

MUGGERIDGE: I'm trying to understand what's going on in the world and that's what you're not doing. You're reacting violently, and you're not trying to understand, you don't understand –

MALE LOYALIST: What do you mean – violently?

MUGGERIDGE: Well, by shouting.

MALE LOYALIST: Mr Muggeridge, today we see two empires in this world: the dollar empire and the Russian empire, and this is what's come through the split up of the British empire.

MUGGERIDGE: I'm trying to explain to you, if you could possibly understand but I'm afraid you can't, that it's not a question of approving of what goes on in the world; it's a question of recognising what goes on in the world –

FEMALE LOYALIST: But we do recognise –

MUGGERIDGE: This is the approach that you're incapable of making, and that's why, although your movement is a completely derisory one, there's a grave danger in the sort of attitude of mind that you have.

MALE LOYALIST: But who derides it?

MUGGERIDGE: I do.

MALE LOYALIST: You do.

MUGGERIDGE: Yes.

MALE LOYALIST: I'd say people like you are a danger, personally.

(All shouting together)

Franchise
I think that the people who don't vote are the absolute flower of our community – they are the élite.

The only candidate I ever wanted to vote for was a man who based his appeal on the fact that, having been confined in a lunatic asylum, he had a certificate of sanity.

Kipling Sahib

An illustrated lecture delivered to the Kipling Society

I remember very vividly, as though it were yesterday, strolling along the Mall in Simla around six o'clock on a November evening thirty-two years ago, and thinking suddenly of Rudyard Kipling with such intense vividness that it almost seemed he was there with me. If one had happened to believe in ghosts, I reflected, his presence in that place would have been in no way surprising. It was Anglo-India in excelsis, and he was the prophet, the chronicler, the poet of Anglo-India, the only one. If he were to walk anywhere, it would surely be there on just such an evening – the distant, majestic Himalayas glowing with the light of the setting sun, and the notes of 'Colonel Bogey', played by a military band in full regalia, sounding so clearly in the crystalline mountain air from the band-stand further along the Mall.

I, too, at that time was working on an Indian newspaper, as Kipling had some half century before. There, I may add, the resemblance ended. Few any longer believed in the Englishman's destiny to rule over palm and pine; least of all me. In the fifty years since Kipling's time the British Raj he extolled had grown tired and feeble, and was soon to come to an end in great bloodshed and ignominy. Yet if posterity ever cares to know about our short-lived conquest of India, one among so many, it is from Kipling's writings alone that they may learn what it was like: from the seeming magnificence of Viceregal power and glory down to Eurasian ticket-collectors, Babu clerks, and the urchin boy, offspring of a drunken Irish trooper who grew up amidst the dust and gossip and squalor of an Indian bazaar: Kim, the embodiment of all Kipling's first fresh delight in the sights and sound and vast diversity of that fantastic land and its diverse, fantastic people. We English have left behind no Taj Mahal to remind the world that once we ruled over India – only a few of our old haunts like Simla: hill stations, clubs, the grounds for polo players and other national idiosyncrasies. If the British Raj is remembered at all, it will be because of Kipling. Artistically speaking he is its single notable product and its only enduring memorial.

Kipling was born in Bombay on 30 December 1865. He spent but seven of his adult years there – 1882 to 1865. Yet, for me, his response to India represented far and away the deepest and most formative experience of all, at any rate as far as his writings were concerned. He positively looked like an Indian (the source of the ridiculous, but widespread rumour that he was really a Eurasian), being sallow and supple, and maturing early for an Anglo-Saxon. He had a moustache while still a schoolboy. If he had never been to India he would have been a totally different person. Perhaps some boring and pedantic don lost in the fastnesses of Eng. Lit., in which he was exceptionally well versed. Or, following a clear bent, one of those tedious maniacs about machines who insist on explaining to all and sundry how the wheels go round. India, it seems to me, in one premature exotic harvest brought out all that was most imaginative and warm and intuitive in him, and, at the same time, planted in him the proneness to adulate power and action – those two black sirens – which so often vulgarised his emotions and distorted his judgements.

It was this aspect of his character which Max Beerbohm found so offensive, and which induced him to draw a particularly cruel cartoon of Kipling. I spoke to Beerbohm about it in Rapallo a year or so before he died, and it visibly saddened him. He regretted the drawing's venom, he said, more particularly as Kipling had gone out of his way to be kind to him when he first began to write.

Still strolling along the Mall in Simla with that so vivid a sense of Kipling's presence upon me, I could project my life as it then was into his when he was working as a journalist in India. The very presses (rotary in my case, flatbed in his) seeming to make their mechanical movements languidly in the sweltering heat; the Indian proof-readers chanting uncomprehendingly the stilted sentences of the next day's paper, like weird priests; the curling galleys, so limp and damp and lifeless, black rivulets of ink spreading over them like the Hoogly's delta, when one made corrections; the punkahs waving to and fro in solemn uselessness, and the insects flying in dark clouds about the lamps, then falling, to pile up in high heaps of transparent holocausted dead. In such circumstances thinking was a slow, laborious business; words had to be laboriously extracted, and arranged with the studied deliberation of a drunk counting his change. Outside, there was the incredible Indian night, so fantastically rich in texture; full of little lights and distant tinkling sounds, and muffled chatter, and shuffling bare footsteps, and alternating whiffs of stench and fragrance which made one's heart stand still. With the paper put to bed, and the presses subsiding into stillness like a heart that stops beating, there was the club to go to; a cavernous place, smelling of cheese and cold beef, where a few mildly tipsy Sahibs in cummerbunds and white coats tried to play billiards watched by inscrutable servants.

Kipling has made a hero, if not a god, of the upper-class Englishman, prototype of the Sahib, such as young George Cottar, the hero of his short story 'The Brushwood Boy', who moves inevitably from public school to Sandhurst.

'His reward was another string of athletic cups, a good-conduct sword, and, at last, Her Majesty's Commission as a subaltern in a first-class line regiment. He did not know that he bore with him from school and college a character worth much fine gold, but was pleased to find his mess so kindly. He had plenty of money of his own; his training had set the public-school mask upon his face, and had taught him how many were the "things no fellow can do". By virtue of the same training he kept his pores open and his mouth shut.'

This excessive adulation led Kipling into transports which now seem almost imbecile. When Cottar Sahib comes on his first home leave from India,

'the house took toll of him, with due regard to precedence – first the mother; then the father; then the housekeeper, who wept and praised God; and then the butler; and so on

89

down to the under-keeper, who had been dog-boy in George's youth, and called him "Master George".'

Finally, his mother comes to tuck him up,

'and they talked for a long hour, as mother and son should, if there is to be any future for our Empire.'

It may be doubted, however, whether Kipling ever managed wholly to acclimatise himself to the Sahibs' India, much as he wanted to. English journalists in his day, even more than in mine, were, hierarchically speaking, of small account. At a Viceregal dinner their place was with the lowliest – among missionaries and even 'natives', as Kipling punctiliously calls Indians who are not so far above him in rank as to be princely, or so far below him as to be droll. The English in India soon followed the example of the Hindus they had conquered, and instituted their own caste system, in which everyone had his due place and status expressed in terms of his salary and the decorations which fell to him.

In Kipling's fragment of autobiography, *Something of Myself*, written in old age, he describes how one evening when he was a young man he was hissed in the Lahore Club. It was an incident which obviously made a deep impression on him. One can imagine how distressed Kipling must have been. He, the laureate of the Sahibs and their Raj, found himself in disfavour in their holy of holies, the Club, with Indian servants witnessing his discomfiture. Whenever the imaginatively gifted turn to glorifying authority, or its janus-face, revolution, they are liable to find themselves in such predicaments. Kipling's recourse was to fall back on the black mystique of action and violence. At the end of *The Light That Failed*, that truly atrocious novel, the hero, Dick Heldar, having gone blind, manages to make his way to the Sudan where he is fortunate enough to hear and smell slaughter before a stray bullet kills him. 'What luck!' he exclaimed. 'What stupendous and imperial luck . . Oh, God has been good to me!'

It was such glorifications of violence and sometimes cruelty in his writings (for Kipling in his life was affectionate, wonderful with children and kindly) which horrified the

more squeamish among his contemporaries. When Andrew
Lang was shown Kipling's story 'The Mark of the Beast',
written in 1800 before its author was known in England, he
described it as 'poisonous stuff', and another – William Sharp

– to whom the manuscript was referred recommended the
instant burning of so detestable a piece of work, and predicted that the author would die mad before the age of thirty.
One sees the point. In 'The Mark of the Beast' an Indian leper

is savagely tortured by two Sahibs, and there is unmistakable relish in the recounting of the episode.

After I returned to England from India in 1936, I went to live in Sussex, a few miles away from Burwash and Kipling's home Bateman's, where he settled in 1903 and spent the last thirty-three years of his life. He, who was by temperament as rootless as Kim, rooted himself with singular tenacity, if not ferocity, in this place, to which he belonged no more than I did. On my own restless walks in the locality, as on the Mall in Simla, I was somehow abnormally conscious of Kipling. There must have been something mediumistic about him which made his physical being extrude from his writings to an unusual, or even abnormal degree. To me, at any rate, his spirit brooded palpably over that countryside which he so brilliantly evoked in his writings.

I recall an evening in early summer by the Rother, with the grazing cows seeming to be afloat on the mist rising over the lush meadowland, heavy with sodden pasture and creamy buttercups. There I saw him – a little dark, spectacled man, so alien a figure, and yet pulling out of the scene its quintessence, his gaze behind the thick spectacle lenses digging deep into the land itself, and excavating out its history.

A portrait of Kipling, as I see it, should be in the medieval style, with a white angel perched on one shoulder and a black devil on the other. The white angel signifies the imagination, out of which come truth and love and laughter; the black devil signifies the will, out of which come rhetoric, hate and portentousness. Kipling was always, it seems to me, in thrall to one or other of those two daemons. He found no peace in the quiet grey twilight between their two kingdoms where most of us reside. All writers are split personalities; literature is a current which flows between the two poles of mysticism and action. Kipling was an extreme case.

It is his memories of India which seem to stir most infallibly the imaginative side of him. Take the case of 'Without Benefit of Clergy'. This marvellous story is about a love affair between a Sahib and an Indian girl who initially has been bought by him for money. Subsequently he falls in love with her, and she bears him a son. To the mother's and his infinite grief the child dies, and then the mother dies in a cholera epidemic, and the Sahib goes disconsolately away muttering to himself: 'Oh, you brute! You utter brute!' One may wonder why, in the circumstances, the Sahib's grief should take so self-condemnatory a form. Is it, I ask myself, because the story relates to some actual experience in Kipling's life? If this were so it might help to account for the curious fact that, though an inveterate traveller, Kipling visited India only once again, for a few days, after he left for England at the age of twenty-four.

Kipling himself managed to see some of the action he so admired in the South African War, when for the first time England came up against a tough opponent, after a series of easy victories against Tibetans, Zulus and other relatively-speaking unarmed fuzzy-wuzzies. Prior to this Kipling's idea of war was largely based on the Indian North-West Frontier – a romantic, but not very dangerous style of fighting which, contrary to Sahib mystique, came to an abrupt end when India achieved independence. Though few recognised it at the time, least of all Kipling, the South African War marked the beginning of the decline of the British Empire, and of the cause of imperialism to which Kipling dedicated his life and work.

In South Africa Kipling made the acquaintance of Cecil Rhodes, and they became, in a manner of speaking, friends. They would sit together in silence for long periods of time, with Rhodes's huge body stretched out on a sofa; then, twisting and turning, he would ask: 'What am I trying to say, Ruddy?' Ruddy might well have retaliated by asking Rhodes: 'What am I trying to do?' They make, it seems to me, a perfect pair – the tubercular giant who became a millionaire on the diamond-fields before he was twenty, and the little short-sighted poet who became world-famous at about the same age.

'What's your dream?' was a question Rhodes was fond of putting. What was Kipling's dream, I wonder? It seems to me he was preoccupied with power in the same sort of way that D. H. Lawrence was preoccupied with sex. In India, when he was there, power was symbolised by the British Raj, and he bowed down before it. Yet in his masterpiece *Kim* the Lama, with his unworldly passion to escape from the Wheel of Life, is the dominant figure, and even Kim finds himself poised between his service to the Raj and to the Lama. Moreover Kipling's veneration for authority as such by no means extended to what we nowadays call the Establishment. He despised, with increasing bitterness, the conduct of affairs under his cousin Stanley Baldwin's premiership; his poem 'Gehazi', about Lord Reading, then Lord Chief Justice, is among the most scorching in the language:

> Stand up, stand up, Gehazi,
> Draw close thy robe and go,
> Gehazi, Judge in Israel,
> A leper white as snow.

He lived to see Gehazi-Reading become Viceroy of India, which must have given a great impetus to the mounting gloom about the prospects for England and the Empire which clouded his latter years. I see him at Bateman's when, as often happened, sleep eluded him, and, as he put it in *Something of Myself*, the night got into his head, shutting him out from the City of Sleep

> Over the edge of the purple down,
> Where the single lamplight gleams,
> Know ye the road to Merciful Town
> That is hard by the Sea of Dreams –
> Where the poor may lay their wrongs away,
> And the sick may forget to weep?
> But we – pity us! Oh pity us! –
> We wakeful; ah pity us! –
> We must go back with Policeman Day –
> Back from the City of Sleep!

It has always seemed extraordinary to me that this strange fancy which Kipling, even as a young man, felt deeply should have been incorporated in a story as otherwise com-

monplace as 'The Brushwood Boy'. Yet there it is – the
dream which came to the Brushwood Boy to solace him in
moments of desolation when the breathless Indian night
seemed to suffocate him; a dream more real than life, also
dreamed in identical terms by the woman he was to marry
before they had made each other's acquaintance. Their
mutual recognition when they met in the flesh made them
realise that love exists before it comes to pass and goes on
existing after it is dead.

Kipling's death in 1936 coincided with King George V's.
There was another less noticed death at the same time – that
of Saklatvala, an Indian Parsee who had become the Communist MP for Battersea. It so happened, as I have read, that
Kipling's cremation followed Saklatvala's, and at the cre-
matorium there was no time to clear away the Red Flags and
other Communist insignia set up for Saklatvala. Truly God is
not mocked.

Hymns
*I think that hymns are very underrated things, that some of the most
exquisite melodies of modern times are hymns; they may well in
the future be as precious to people as border ballads were.*

Pilgrims to Lourdes

A journey with the sick

The departure platform has a different air from the others. The departing are pilgrims, many of them sick. For them travelling presents particular difficulties. They are not holiday-makers in the ordinary sense. They are bound not for a beach or a resort, but for a shrine – Saint Bernadette's, the most popular Christian cult of modern times. The sick and the crippled make the arduous journey in the hope of a miracle. The others who are whole and well help with the disabled, and look to receive spiritual edification themselves. I find so outrageous a defiance of the twin contemporary gods of science and pleasure very much to my taste.

On this train the sick are the centre of attention – not shunned as they tend to be in our humanitarian societies, where they remind us of the fallibility of all human endeavours. Thinking about it, it's an extraordinary thing that in the middle of the twentieth century there should be this great load of people, some sick and some well, some old and some young, hoping to some degree, consciously or unconsciously, for a miracle. I thought that travelling with so many sick people, and some of them very sick, would be depressing. Actually it's not. There's a terrific atmosphere of an outing. And of course when you think about it, quite apart from any hopes of being made physically better, if you spend your days in a hospital bed, or incapacitated, a trip to Lourdes, on any showing, is a lift to the spirits. One dreads to sentimentalise men and women so afflicted. I need not have worried. They are easy to talk to, and disarm mawkish pity by their robust attitude to their misfortunes.

MAN WITH CRUTCHES: I'm suffering from disseminated sclerosis, it's a brain disease sort of thing, which affects the

96

walking and movements of the legs.

MUGGERIDGE: Makes it more difficult to get around?

MAN: Yes, I can't get around without sticks and I go very slowly.

MUGGERIDGE: And you're hoping at Lourdes to throw these sticks away?

MAN: I'm hoping to wrap them around somebody's neck.

MUGGERIDGE: I give you full permission to wrap them around my neck. If you don't get a miracle will you still have been glad to come?

MAN: I will indeed because I think it's very spiritually refreshing.

MUGGERIDGE: What's that mean?

MAN: Well, refreshing from the point of view of the hereafter sort of thing.

Rolling across the plains of France the pilgrims have their rosaries, their prayers, their offices, and their friends and helpers to sustain and solace them. Whether hopes of heaven are well- or ill-founded I do not know; but certainly they help to make earthly misfortunes more bearable..

MUGGERIDGE: Tell us why you are going to Lourdes.

QUADRAPLEGIC PILGRIM ON TRAIN: Well I'm going to Lourdes primarily because I believe strongly that it is possible for a miracle to occur, not necessarily to me but to someone in the pilgrimage some time. But if it doesn't, it doesn't make any difference at all – one is strengthened spiritually, and even physically in a sense, because one is able to go on with one's life as it is. And you get a renewal of strength.

MUGGERIDGE: This happened to you when you went before?

PILGRIM: Yes, I found a great improvement. In fact before this present pilgrimage my mother remarked that she found an improvement in me, generally, after being at Lourdes. I was very much worse than I am now, but I did improve physically.

MUGGERIDGE: Have you always been bedridden like this?

PILGRIM: Yes, from birth.

MUGGERIDGE: Do you think a miracle might happen to you?

PILGRIM: Well, I think it is possible. Not necessarily to me but to someone. It could happen to me with the mercy of God. I really believe that God is almighty, and that is not just a figure of speech, but in fact He is almighty.

I was never before on quite such a journey as this one, now nearing its destination. So harrowing, and yet so cheerful. What a waste of time, effort and expense, it might be urged, to transport these unfortunates so far; and yet, looked at in another way, how infinitely worth while for them and all concerned.

The pilgrims' destination is the Domain within the town of Lourdes, where the cult of Bernadette is practised. It's devised almost like a stage set. At all times and seasons pilgrims come in tens of thousands, of all races, nationalities and classes, but mostly poor and humble, to pray, join processions, meditate, and, as they hope, to commune with their saint. The place is never still, and never empty; drama is endlessly enacted – of blessings and mercies ardently beseeched, and of misfortunes and disappointments meekly endured. One has to come to the grotto where Bernadette is reputed to have had her vision either very early in the morning, or very late at night, to find it other than crowded. At those times it really does, in some mysterious way, give one a sense of being in a holy place, if only because of the millions and millions of people who come and worship here, in all seasons and at all times. Even on a rainy morning there is a crowd of worshippers clustered round the grotto. What, I ask myself, brings them there? I should say hope, hope of better health, for a stronger faith, for their soul's salvation maybe, or for more trivial mundane things – like easier circumstances, and fulfilled ambition. Not only, or even particularly, for themselves but for those they love. It's easy to ridicule acceptance of the magical qualities of this place and of the waters of the spring people drink and bathe in. One can look with a sceptical eye at the rather unconvincing display of crutches allegedly cast aside by cripples who've been miraculously cured. I find no such inclination myself. It seems to me in all sincerity, and even humility, that these Lourdes pilgrims – mostly very humble lowly people – may have had a clearer and even more practical vision than other traffickers in hope in our time, like psychiatrists and advertisers, and travellers to the moon.

The grotto where Bernadette is reputed to have had her vision is, of course, above all where the pilgrims want to be. They go there eagerly and leave reluctantly: ravaged, patient faces endlessly passing. Who dare say that they should be deprived of this so precarious hope in favour of another, ostensibly better founded, in the shape of a coloured capsule, a sharp knife, some human disentangling of their human ills? Certainly not I. The water from the grotto, eagerly swallowed, medically speaking probably does as much, or as little good as any other medicine.

Although the Lourdes weather is notoriously changeable – close and overcast, and unsuitable for the sick – the pilgrims cheerfully take their meals, whenever possible, in the open air.

MUGGERIDGE: Doctor, I imagine that you would have to select, to some extent, people who could undertake a journey like this?

DOCTOR: Yes, we do have a regular series of selection committees, and they have to get very special certificates from their own doctors, telling us about the disease, and as to whether they are really fit to travel.

MUGGERIDGE: Of course, in a way to say they weren't fit to travel would be in itself a sort of contradiction of the thing.

DOCTOR: Yes, of course a lot of people do try to swing it – they do get away with murder – but we are prepared to take people who are pretty well near dying. We have facilities for taking stretcher cases, and in actual fact, as it turns out every now and then, one perhaps two, even one year three people died here. They came on those conditions really. If they're dying, it's their lot anyway. They're most of them pretty ill. There's only one end to illness, unless they're cured unexpectedly.

MUGGERIDGE: Are they – I mean, would it be true to say that the majority of cases here are from a medical point of view hopeless cases?

DOCTOR: I should think so, certainly 80% of them are – they've been ill for – usually many years. They're not going to get better unless something unexpected happens.

MUGGERIDGE: And this something unexpected means a miracle?

DOCTOR: Yes, that's in the theological sense. In the medical sense of course we don't talk of miracles, we talk of 'inexplicable cures' – cures that are not explainable by natural means.

MUGGERIDGE: Have you yourself witnessed a miracle?

DOCTOR: No. Miracles are few and far between.

MUGGERIDGE: What happens – I mean in your opinion as a doctor – what happens when one of these miracles takes place?

DOCTOR: Well the sort of miracles that happen at Lourdes are usually normal cures, with one unexplained factor, and that is that they occur instantaneously.

MUGGERIDGE: Doctor, one last point I'd very much like to put to you is whether there's any real point in protracting the life of people in such a sorry state as they are. What do you feel about that as a doctor?

DOCTOR: Well, we've had people coming here year after year. I've one man in mind: gradually from coming in a chair he was brought on a stretcher; and he gradually curled up and the only sign of intelligence in him was a twinkle in his eye. He had to be fed, he had to have everything done for him, he could just swallow. And he'd look at you and make a sort of ugly leer, but when you saw him, when you saw his whole face, you realised how beautiful his smile was, and poor old Jock, he lived a full life right to the very end.

Particular importance is attached to bathing in the waters of the grotto. Outside the baths the pilgrims wait their turn for a dip. It is a very ancient notion that bodily and spiritually imperfections may be washed away like dirt in clear water. I think of the Ganges at Benares black with bathers; of the leper who emerged from bathing with his flesh cured and wholesome. Willing hands, to the accompaniment of intoned prayers, dip battered bodies into the water from Bernadette's spring. Magic? Superstition? Sublime faith? Something of all three I expect. At any rate, for the battered bodies at least some refreshment, one hopes.

In Lourdes it goes without saying that the Roman Catholic Church is present all the time. The streets throng with monks and nuns and ecclesiastics of varying orders and degrees. The air is full of the sound of prayers being intoned, and of hymns and anthems being sung. In the Middle Ages I suppose it would all have seemed natural enough, but to a twentieth-century mind, bruised and battered by the ferocious currents of our time, it seems more disconcerting and even alarming. Though I hasten to add that the music is magnificently evocative and like the prayers still conveys, as was originally intended, the longing for perfection of hearts intrinsically imperfect. In such circumstances it's natural, as it were, to stand apart and look at this ancient faith moving in so dramatically opposite a direction to the pursuit of happiness in terms of affluence and sensual satisfaction on which the bulk of mankind today seem to be so ardently bent. Is it a dying echo of a splendid but now abolished past? Or does it still enshrine the only valid answer to the confusions and conflicts of an age like ours, one of the cruellest of history, and at the same time, materially speaking, one of the most fabulously successful. I have to admit that I personally alternate from one view to the other. But this I can truthfully say: the pilgrims who come to Lourdes do seem to derive from the offices of the Church a spiritual strength to face their misfortunes with fortitude and even at times exultation. Stretched out in their wheelchairs and their stretchers, to await a blessing that won't cure their stricken flesh – they still have quite a festive air, compared with psychiatric wards, where the children of affluence rage and fret.

Each afternoon a procession forms. For the sick, wheeled into position in front of the Basilica, this is the day's awesome moment, when, if at all, their anguished prayers will be answered. It is infinitely touching to see mothers carefully manoeuvring their children into position to be as near as possible to the Host when it passes. This, of all times, is when a miracle might happen. Perhaps today . . . perhaps today some desperate and humanly incurable malady will pass; an inhuman look be made human; God's handiwork restored. Perhaps today. . . .

MUGGERIDGE: I was thinking, when I watched you going round in the procession, that there were those people stretched out, and they hear the words from the priest 'God can cure you', and I thought perhaps if I'd been lying there, being an impatient and worldly sort of person, I should think, Well, why doesn't He?

BISHOP: Why doesn't God cure all the sick in the world? Surely this is to infringe on God's domain and to plan people's lives as we would wish them planned, not as He would wish them planned. And none of us can say that we share in divine wisdom to that extent, can we? We are very proud of our planning, we plan the political and social issues of this world. Do they always turn out to be wise plans? Isn't it absolutely necessary for us to try to conform our minds with the mind of God, to try and see His designs, His plans? If a person is not cured physically, it doesn't follow that that sick person hasn't a very definite purpose in life.

Bernadette is looked to for help – touching her rock, like touching a loving face, beseechingly. It is a rock like any other rock geologically speaking; the water under scientific analysis indubitably H_2O. Yet not to the pilgrims. To them a rock of ages cleft for them; the water a rare and precious balm of great worth. Lourdes itself is as dedicated to the pilgrims as Stratford-upon-Avon is to Shakespeare. Some find the souvenirs offered for sale in such numbers repugnant. They are not very appealing, but I daresay inevitable. In any case, they don't appear to trouble the pilgrims, who for the most part are too poor to be other than meagre purchasers.

To most people Lourdes signifies the sick and the dying, and they do, it must be said, loom large in this place. Sometimes one sees them with a certain disquiet and even distaste, as extras brought on and off the stage in a macabre way, in the presentation of a Christian morality play. At other times, their cheerful fortitude seems a particular glory, and puts to shame one's own complaining about ills so incomparably less exacting. The question inevitably poses itself as to whether these maimed, stunted lives should be protracted, and, in the case of congenital defects, ever begun. Can these poor souls, one asks oneself, sometimes in outward appearance barely human, really wish to go on living? The scientific answer, of course, is emphatically no. In a broiler house, there's no place for such poor specimens. They are, to use a particularly odious expression, useless mouths. But then, our world is not a broiler house, though alas, as we've seen, it can easily be made one. If the Christian view is correct, and mankind are a family, with a Father in Heaven who can't see even a sparrow fall to the ground without concern, then these twisted, tangled bodies have as rightful a place in the human family as any others, even when they can scarcely utter their insistence that life has been to them a precious gift, and they duly offer thanks to their Maker for it. I, as it happens, believe them more readily than I do the pronouncements of experts on population and eugenics. It can be argued, it seems to me, that no lives are worth living, or that all lives are worth living, but not that some lives are worth living and others not.

In the torchlight procession the little candles separately carried make one pattern to the accompaniment of one melody. The faces pass like shadows, and I watched them pass, envious perhaps of their serenity, and of the certainty which shines in their candles. So many hearts which might legitimately be uplifted, with their ever ardent endlessly repeated 'Ave Marias'.

Such is Lourdes. With the pilgrimage over the pilgrims

return, little if at all better in body, but surely heartened and strengthened to face a continuance of that other unremitting pilgrimage – their daily lives.

MUGGERIDGE: What are your impressions now of the pilgrimage that we went on together there?

QUADRAPLEGIC PILGRIM: It's almost like a second heaven; everybody seems to be thinking of one thing, that is the worship of God, and the fellowship of the other sick pilgrims is wonderful. To be there at all is a miracle for me.

MUGGERIDGE: Has it made you feel better?

PILGRIM: It's made me feel that I have nothing at all to worry about. In comparison with other people, I have a home, I've got people to look after me, my mother – we do everything together – and when I think of the suffering of the others, mine is a very little cross.

MUGGERIDGE: Do you feel physically better for your pilgrimage?

PILGRIM: Yes, I think in a slight way my legs are not so stiff as they were.

MUGGERIDGE: But did you hope?

PILGRIM: One always hopes.

MUGGERIDGE: Are you disappointed that nothing more dramatic happened to you?

PILGRIM: No, I'm not, because I said when I went there that if it was God's will to do this for me He would do it. One can ask, but one cannot demand.

Current Reflections

This film made a greater impression on me than any other television programme I'd ever been concerned with, not so much because of Lourdes itself but its implications. Ultimately what one cannot avoid thinking about endlessly is why human beings have to suffer as they do. This is a place of suffering. Yet you see people who have overcome suffering to a great extent, and it was then that I began to understand clearly how suffering is an integral part of human life, and that the cross, symbol of the Christian religion, has made this enormous impression on history, because that is its message.

Wail On

I attended the military parade in Jerusalem to mark the Israeli takeover of the whole city – the first time for many centuries that a Jewish army had been in charge in Jerusalem. On such an occasion the Wailing Wall was a place one instinctively made for. The Rabbis were out in force, all wailing away. 'Why wail now?' I asked a man in a white cap standing near me, 'Oughtn't they to be throwing their fur hats in the air?' 'There's always plenty to wail about,' he answered sternly. 'So there is, so there is,' I agreed.

Lord Reith Looks Back

John Reith, first Director-General of the BBC, was born in Scotland in 1889. Youngest son of the Minister of the College Church, Glasgow, he was brought up in the strict religious atmosphere of the Manse. On leaving school he served an apprenticeship as a locomotive engineer. He joined up on the outbreak of the First World War, and, as a lieutenant, was severely wounded in France in 1915.

In 1922 he joined the BBC as General Manager. After shaping and directing it for fifteen years he resigned, hoping that he would be called upon to play a significant role in the conduct of the war he knew was coming. He became Chairman of Imperial Airways, and a few months later he formed BOAC as a public Corporation and was its first Chairman. In the early years of the war he was successively Minister of Information, Minister of Transport and the first Minister of Works, under Chamberlain and then Churchill. Subsequently he joined the RNVR, becoming Director of Combined Operations Material – a department of the Admiralty which, characteristically, he invented himself, and which played an important part in the D-Day landings. He was knighted in 1927 and created Baron Reith of Stonehaven in 1940.

The Early Years

MUGGERIDGE: Were you a bright student?

REITH: No.

MUGGERIDGE: But you were interested in your studies weren't you?

REITH: I was interested, but I had no stimulus to excel. I got through examinations too easily.

MUGGERIDGE: Games?

REITH: Rugby in particular, rugby football. Quite early on I was moved from forward to take the place of the full back who'd been hurt. I never moved from the full back position.

MUGGERIDGE: That suited you.

REITH: That suited me. Can you see something in that?

MUGGERIDGE: Yes I can. I can see that as a forward you were one of a pack, and you couldn't really stand up in a pack too much. As a back you would put up individual performance.

REITH: Absolutely, and one was an establishment of one's own, so to speak.

MUGGERIDGE: I've read that you used to go walking when you were young, in the dark with the wind blowing, and that's where you felt yourself to be isolated?

REITH: Yes I was trying to determine what I was meant to do in the world, feeling that I was meant to do something, not just to be a mediocrity.

MUGGERIDGE: But why isolated? That's what I don't understand.

REITH: You mean lonely?

MUGGERIDGE: Lonely.

REITH: Yes, very lonely.

MUGGERIDGE: Without friends, without intimates?

REITH: Very, very few friends indeed.

MUGGERIDGE: Now why was that?

REITH: Possibly I wasn't a friendly character myself.

MUGGERIDGE: Or perhaps this feeling of having some tremendous destiny of your own?

REITH: Maybe. Bit arrogant, isn't it?

MUGGERIDGE: I don't know. It's a thing that some men have had, this feeling. When you write about it, it's as though the wind had so much to do with your thoughts.

REITH: Ah yes, particularly when it came nor-westerly or northerly.

MUGGERIDGE: Now why should that be?

REITH: From Ben Lomond and the hills running at the beginning of the Grampian Range. I used to think, you know, particularly when there was a wind and a sound of music in the trees, that there was a message for me, but I couldn't quite make it out, couldn't quite make it out.

MUGGERIDGE: Never caught it.

REITH: Never caught it. A job on your own.

MUGGERIDGE: But I still can't quite see what was going on in your head.

REITH: A struggle to find guidance, guidance from my own self I suppose, if I couldn't get it from others, as to what one was to do.

MUGGERIDGE: Were you tremendously ambitious?

REITH: I was tremendously over-serious, I think. I doubt if I've ever been young. I don't think I took the potential enjoyment of life as most people of my age would and did.

MUGGERIDGE: Because you were too serious?

REITH: I was inordinately ambitious, I suppose, to be fully stretched, which is a word I've been asked to explain before, to be fully stretched; inordinately ambitious to be of service.

MUGGERIDGE: Ambition must have been directed into certain concrete forms, mustn't it? You must have wanted to be this or that.

REITH: No. Because, deplorably, I couldn't make up my mind as to what I wanted to do. I left school with a vague feeling that I wanted to go to Oxford or Cambridge for Classics. You know what Robert Louis Stevenson said about engineering? The most arduous form of idleness. Nobody can talk to me about hours of work or about the care in turning out a job. Getting up at a quarter to five in the morning, a fifty-six-hour week and quite often overtime. And three-hour evening classes almost every night.

MUGGERIDGE: It's fascinating for me to speculate if you'd gone to Oxford instead of Glasgow, because I loathe Oxford myself.

REITH: Well switch over to Cambridge.

MUGGERIDGE: I hate that even more. I feel that if you'd gone and been subjected to that very insidious kind of brainwashing that these older universities go in for, you wouldn't have been this man that you are, and I think much less.

REITH: I hear you.

MUGGERIDGE: Going back——

REITH: Did you get what I said just now?

MUGGERIDGE: You said, I hear you.

REITH: That's typical Scots.

MUGGERIDGE: What does it signify?

REITH: I hear you. Meaning that the remark is not worth answering or that the remark that had been made was untrue. I hear you. You never heard that?

MUGGERIDGE: I never heard it. Would you say that you had, when you were a student, a fairly clear set of values that you had accepted and that therefore dominated the way you looked at life and the way you thought of living?

REITH: Yes.

MUGGERIDGE: If you had to say in a few words what it is, what would you say it was?

REITH: A passionate desire for truth in oneself, one's actions, in one's believing. Kindness.

MUGGERIDGE: Meaning sympathy, understanding in dealing with other human beings. What's called love.

REITH: I haven't used that word love particularly. I have particularly avoided using that word.

MUGGERIDGE: Why?

REITH: Because it's awfully misused. You know the lines from Burns –

> If we had'na loved so kindly,
> If we had'na loved so blindly,
> Never met, nor ever parted,
> We had ne'er been broken hearted.

That's one kind of love, isn't it?

MUGGERIDGE: Yes. Marvellous. Do you have such regrets in your own life?

REITH: No, not of a particular act. If you want to follow up and press me and embarrass me more, you will say, 'Were you thinking of a particular individual?'

MUGGERIDGE: Well, I do say it.

REITH: And if I said no, you wouldn't believe me.

MUGGERIDGE: I wouldn't.

REITH: Well then, I don't say anything.

MUGGERIDGE: You've got to say yes.

REITH: I've got the last word.

MUGGERIDGE: That's a brilliant evasion, because I can't proceed any further. But of course the truth is that I don't think anybody could live to be your age or mine without some experiences which those lines would in some way convey. Isn't that true?

REITH: I hear you.

The BBC

MUGGERIDGE: When you saw that famous advertisement for a General Manager of the British Broadcasting Company and you went into that place in Kingsway, did something tell you that this was the end of the quest?

REITH: Before that. It was very odd. One evening in Regent Square Presbyterian Church the Minister, Dr Ivan Robin, preached a sermon about the Lord requiring a man to fill up a gap, and he said, 'Maybe there's somebody in this congregation tonight that might be called to fill a considerable gap'. Extraordinary thing. . . . And this entry in my diary finished the day, 'I still believe there is some great work for me to do in the world'. And I found the BBC, or the BBC found me.

MUGGERIDGE: Tell us how it happened. Because it's a strange enough chance.

REITH: An advertisement in the *Morning Post* one day. British Broadcasting Company: Applications are invited for the following offices: General Manager, Secretary, Director of Programmes, Chief Engineer. Only those with first-class qualifications need apply. I wrote an application in the Cavendish Club, and then I did what I ought to have done before, looked up the name of the man this advertisement said would receive the applications. Having seen his name in

111

Who's Who, I then went to the hall porter and persuaded him to allow me to recover this letter, and I added a P.S. – 'No doubt you would know some of my people in Aberdeen'. And that is why I got the job.

MUGGERIDGE: And why the BBC became what it did become. Because you shaped it, didn't you?

REITH: I suppose I did.

MUGGERIDGE: Well of course you did. I can't get it out of mind, this picture of you, a young man coming to London from Scotland not so very long before, suddenly confronted with this enormous responsibility and accepting it. Did you never have doubts? Did you never think: Am I really qualified to exercise this incredible authority?

REITH: No. No, I don't – no, definitely not. I was going to say, no I don't think so, but I'll withdraw that and say definitely not.

MUGGERIDGE: And where did the certainty and the confidence come from?

REITH: Well, you would say it was derivative of self-confidence. An unjustified self-confidence maybe. I just felt I could – mark you, with the help of the Almighty, and I say that seriously, I mean it absolutely, however I might describe it. I would say that the Almighty was there in my receiving that job and was there with me in my execution of the job. Have you got anything to say about that?

MUGGERIDGE: The only thing I'd say is this, that of course the ordinary person listening to that, not knowing you particularly well, would think: Surely a man who has as close a relation with the Almighty as that should have a certain humility, and that this is perhaps lacking.

REITH: Now you've got me on that.

MUGGERIDGE: You realised what an enormous thing the BBC was going to be, that it was going to change people's lives. How did you shape to the task of dealing with it?

REITH: With complete confidence. Is that the answer?

MUGGERIDGE: One part. Didn't it ever worry you to think that the logical outcome of the way you were looking at the future of broadcasting was to be, in effect, a monopoly?

REITH: No. I'd have been very worried otherwise. There were criticisms of the monopoly position before we started. I would say that they almost entirely disappeared within three or four years.

MUGGERIDGE: Well, honesty compels me to admit that I was one of the critics myself, and I was a critic because I thought that, however admirably conducted a monopoly might be, it would always in the end operate on the side of the established social order. Isn't that true?

REITH: I wouldn't admit that the BBC was operated by me on the side of the Establishment.

MUGGERIDGE: In essential points.

REITH: Do you mean political, moral?

MUGGERIDGE: I mean in every way. I mean you in all good faith upheld a social system, a church, a government's policy – in all good faith, and there's no reason on earth why you shouldn't. But I see in that the danger of a monopoly.

REITH: Technically, I thought a monopoly was justifiable, but I was far, far more interested in the monopoly in terms of the intellectual and ethical standard of the content of its programmes.

MUGGERIDGE: That would imply that the ethical standard and the intellectual standard which you decided upon was to be the prevailing standard.

REITH: Yes. Arrogant?

MUGGERIDGE: Self-confident.

REITH: Self-confident?

MUGGERIDGE: In the sense that you'd feel that you were equipped to decide that. It has been said that when you picked your staff, you satisfied yourself that they were Christians and that their way of life was, in the conventional sense, respectable.

113

REITH: It's a lovely story. It's partly true.

MUGGERIDGE: I bet you'd never have appointed me, for instance! If I'd applied.

REITH: Don't be too sure. People used to say that I put them through the mangle. Have you ever been put through the mangle?

MUGGERIDGE: In my day.

REITH: If a man was going to be concerned with the ethical side, as in talks and so forth, I was interested to know what his views were on religion. I never said 'You must be a Christian'. I asked their views. And got their views. I mean, if a man were considerably like-minded to myself obviously one would still read his reference carefully, but one would know that basically we were out for the same thing.

Political Pressures

MUGGERIDGE: I'd like to talk about one incident relating to your position vis-à-vis the Government: and that was the General Strike. Up to that point you'd had a relationship with the Government which had never really been tested?

REITH: Not seriously.

MUGGERIDGE: Now it is tested seriously.

REITH: It came on us all of a sudden, but we had two or three days' warning and we were, to a considerable extent, prepared for it. I lived quite near the Abbey then, which meant that one was easily available to the Houses of Parliament, and I got the newspaper leader in my house which started the thing – the *Daily Mail* leader, do you remember?

MUGGERIDGE: Yes I remember; which the printers refused to print.

REITH: I got the Prime Minister's view about the thing, and I suppose the Cabinet's view soon after that, and I myself broadcast those from my ordinary telephone in 6 Barton Street all over the country, because by that time all the transmitters were connected to headquarters. I had an interview with the Prime Minister the next morning. Stanley Baldwin was on the other side of the table, walking up and down, smoking a pipe, and I was making a passionate appeal that the Government should leave the BBC alone, and trust to me. And he said to me, 'Actually, I'm going to put this to the Cabinet in terms of trusting the Managing Director. Is that all right!' I said, 'Yes, fine.' Well, there were grumbles. The Cabinet weren't happy about this; there was a division. The majority accepted it, the minority, in particular Churchill and Birkenhead, didn't like it. Hundreds of people already knew that the big power station down the road was out of action, hundreds and thousands possibly, and the BBC broadcast the fact. Churchill fulminated about that, broadcasting the success of the strikers. Do you see the point?

MUGGERIDGE: Yes, I do. He, in other words, wanted the BBC taken over by the Government to become an organ of propaganda, is that right?

REITH: Absolutely.

MUGGERIDGE: And you resisted that?

REITH: I passed every single news bulletin. We were broadcasting news about the success of the strikers in particular, actions where far more harm would have been caused if we hadn't, and Churchill wouldn't or couldn't – couldn't or wouldn't – see that, and to the every end he kept up his grumbling in the Cabinet, and with Stanley Baldwin. Now Ramsay MacDonald, who was Leader of the Opposition, asked me if I would allow the Archbiship of Canterbury to speak. I had a letter delivered by hand from the Archbishop enclosing what he wanted to say. It was just an appeal to the Government to be – as the Archbishop thought, I suppose – generous and large-minded, and not stand on the letter of the law. So I sent it along to Baldwin, and was told, 'The Prime Minister would rather you didn't do that'. Do you get the terminology?

MUGGERIDGE: Oh yes.

REITH: We'd rather you didn't do it, and there was I, you see, in the invidious position of having to arbitrate between the Prime Minister of the country and the Archbishop of Canterbury, because I was so frightened of what Churchill would make of it – get me?

MUGGERIDGE: Yes.

REITH: So I told the Archbishop I was sorry I wouldn't agree to his broadcasting. Was I right? I think I was right, but I hated it. I think the Prime Minister was mistaken.

MUGGERIDGE: I can see exactly why you did it, but at the same time you have to recognise that it's things like that which have led people to say that in the last resort the BBC has to accept the Government's direction.

Television

MUGGERIDGE: Did you see the potentialities of television from the beginning? Did you see what an enormous thing it was going to become?

REITH: I was frightened of it from the start.

MUGGERIDGE: Now why exactly?

REITH: There's an admission. Do you need to ask why?

MUGGERIDGE: I'd like to know.

REITH: You know yourself. And you could describe it better than I. May I ask you a question?

MUGGERIDGE: Yes, of course.

REITH: Has the introduction of television been to the benefit or the hurt of this country, of the world?

MUGGERIDGE: I would find that a terribly difficult thing to answer, particularly for me personally, because most of the great inventions of our time arouse in my mind at best a question mark. But now we come to the most extraordinary moment of all. You've created this great organisation. You're in a position of very great authority, one of the three or four most powerful people of this country, and suddenly you walk out.

REITH: Look, I thought I had got a good organisation, one

that would stand up to anything, including war, including the development of television. In other words, I felt I was going to be to an extent unemployed, certainly not fully stretched, and I was frightened of that.

MUGGERIDGE: Your work was finished there?

REITH: My work was finished, provided always they chose the right man to succeed me.

MUGGERIDGE: Do you think that what you did was the right thing to do, or a mistake?

REITH: A frightful mistake.

MUGGERIDGE: You should have stayed?

REITH: Yes.

MUGGERIDGE: And you made the mistake for the sake of this phrase that you use a tremendous lot in your writing and in talking, of being 'fully stretched'.

REITH: Yes, of every sort, physical and mental. Anyhow mental, particularly mental.

MUGGERIDGE: With no, as it were, slack at all?

REITH: Very, very little.

MUGGERIDGE: Is that really a sensible way to live?

REITH: No.

MUGGERIDGE: But it's your way.

REITH: I never learnt to live. You never believe me.

MUGGERIDGE: No, I don't. But that's an extraordinary thing to say – that you never learnt to live?

REITH: I mean it.

MUGGERIDGE: But it's——

REITH: Look – I did not realise until too late that life was for living. Now is that a bit clearer?

MUGGERIDGE: Did you actually just walk out of the BBC?

REITH: I stopped a presentation. I stopped anything by way of a farewell. My wife came for me, and we went down in the lift from the third floor, and across the hall to the entrance, or

117

in this instance the exit, and there was standing the Senior Commissionaire who'd been on duty for the company ever since it had started. My wife drew back there, went over and shook hands with him. A simple action. Too much for me. Beat me completely, and I went out of Broadcasting House, tears running down my cheeks. Then I did the most ridiculous, macabre sort of journey round the countryside with two or three of the senior people whom I knew best. We had dinner at Droitwich, and after dinner, late dinner it was, very late, we went to the high-powered transmitters there, and I myself shut down the engines at midnight, and they asked me to sign my name in the book, the Visitors' Book, and I did. 'J. C. W. Reith, ex-BBC.'

Churchill

MUGGERIDGE: When the war came, Chamberlain offered you the Ministry of Information and without much enthusiasm you took it.

REITH: Yes.

MUGGERIDGE: You were to be our Goebbels.

REITH: Yes. That's what one was meant to be and ought to have been if one could only get the confidence of the Prime Minister.

MUGGERIDGE: Then in came Churchill.

REITH: In came Churchill.

MUGGERIDGE: And what happened then?

REITH: Walter Monckton and I were listening one night in the Ministry to a news bulletin and among the news items was that Mr Duff Cooper was appointed Minister of Information.

MUGGERIDGE: This was the first you heard, as Minister of Information. Incredible.

REITH: All right. Now, I waited for two or three days and then I was sent for by Churchill. And he looked among his papers and he said, 'Oh, but I-I-I, well, there's something I want you to do.' He looked among the papers, you see, to find what it was he wanted me to do. 'I want you to go to the Ministry of Transport.' I said, 'All right, sir.'

MUGGERIDGE: Do you think that Churchill was hostile to you as a result of your previous disagreements when you were in the BBC?

REITH: Yes, he was. We were at a distance, there was no doubt about that. I saw him very, very occasionally. I was hardly aware of a Prime Minister through my term in the Ministry of Transport and the nearly two years, or whatever it was, in the Ministry of Works, hardly aware of a Prime Minister.

MUGGERIDGE: Did you like him? I mean putting everything else aside.

REITH: No, I didn't. I disliked him – I think I disliked him very much indeed.

MUGGERIDGE: I see from your journal that you had an exchange of letters with Churchill after the war.

REITH: Yes.

MUGGERIDGE: And you explained to him various things. This is what you put in the last paragraph. 'I have, like you, a war mentality, and other qualities which should have commended themselves to you. Even in office I was nothing like fully stretched and I was completely out of touch with you. You could have used me in a way, and to an extent, you never realised. Instead of that there's been the sterility, humiliation and distress of all these years, eyeless in Gaza, without even the consolation Samson had in knowing it was his own fault, and that's how and where I still am.' That's your letter.

REITH: That's a good paragraph, isn't it?

MUGGERIDGE: Not bad. I see you got a telegram acknowledging it.

REITH: Oh, did I?

MUGGERIDGE: Now this is his letter to you, which is also extremely interesting. 'So far as my administration's concerned, I've always admired your abilities and energy and it was with regret that I was not able to include you in the considerable reconstruction of the Government in February 1942. Several times since then I've considered you for various posts which became vacant, but I always encountered considerable opposition from one quarter or another on the grounds that you were difficult to work with . . . If you think I can be of service to you at any time, pray let me know, for I'm very sorry that the fortunes of war should have proved so adverse to you, and I feel the state is in your debt.'

REITH: Good letter.

MUGGERIDGE: Yes.

REITH: But when he became Prime Minister again, he didn't do anything to discharge the debt of the state.

MUGGERIDGE: Isn't that always the case with politics?

REITH: Too often.

MUGGERIDGE: Putting aside the question of Churchill as a war leader, what do you think about him as a Prime Minister?

REITH: Do you want me to answer that?

MUGGERIDGE: Yes I do.

REITH: Ought I to?

MUGGERIDGE: I'm absolutely sure you ought to.

REITH: I doubt if England will recover from Churchill. Anyhow not for a long time. He gave no moral lead whatever after the war, when the country was as badly in need of it as it was during the war. I'm not talking now about Churchill as the wartime Prime Minister. I'm talking about him – in your terms – as an ordinary Prime Minister coming back. He gave no moral lead whatever. I would add this. Something has got to be done to put that right, and then the country may, I hope will, recover, and surely we ought to believe it can and will.

MUGGERIDGE: Would I be right in saying that the principles of democracy applied in a particular institution or in a society are not particularly dear to you? Would I be right?

REITH: No. By and large, no, because this is what I would say, that I think on the whole I approve of study and endeavour to achieve the principles of a democracy, but the processes – my golly – no.

MUGGERIDGE: In a word, what do you think is the best form of government?

REITH: Despotism tempered by assassination.

MUGGERIDGE: Is that what you had in the BBC when you were the boss?

REITH: Absolutely not. I had a most excellent and appreciated form of paternalism. Is that bad?

MUGGERIDGE: But no assassination?

REITH: No assassination – not that I was aware of.

MUGGERIDGE: There might have been a little here and there.

REITH: I believe profoundly in paternalism.

MUGGERIDGE: Yes, I know.

REITH: I am often – this is getting a bit personal – but I am often accused of having been autocratic and dictatorial, and all the rest of it in the BBC. Was my management unkind, cruel? Or wicked in any way?

MUGGERIDGE: It's a terribly difficult question for me to answer because I wasn't there. But there are people who think it was.

REITH: Cruel?

MUGGERIDGE: They think that it was – intolerant.

REITH: Intolerance is not necessarily cruelty.

MUGGERIDGE: But it can easily become it, can't it?

REITH: Yes. Well, did it become it with me?

MUGGERIDGE: I don't think of you as a cruel man at all. But I think of you as a man who is prepared in the interests of efficiency to be autocratic.

REITH: Oh yes.

MUGGERIDGE: And I think that's a dangerous position. I think that's why when the devil tempted Christ, offered Him the Kingdoms of the earth, he very wisely turned them down. But you would have accepted them.

REITH: Maybe I would, maybe not.

Values

MUGGERIDGE: You regard your career as the story of a failure. Most people would regard it as a fantastic success story. Why do you consider it to be a failure?

REITH: Of course this is awfully embarrassing, but let me just put one point to you. Can anyone really judge of success or failure other than the man or the woman concerned?

MUGGERIDGE: You mean that it has to be a subjective judgement.

REITH: All right, yes.

MUGGERIDGE: You said earlier on 'I haven't really lived. I've never learnt to live.' Now, I've puzzled and puzzled over this and I still don't really know what you mean by it.

REITH: Do you remember I said I'd never been young?

MUGGERIDGE: Yes.

REITH: That's the beginning of the explanation. And I suppose most of the rest of the explanation is that one has been far too serious-minded, far too desirous of getting the paper off the table quick. I've had awfully few holidays in my life. Now that's sheer stupidity – lack of proportion.

MUGGERIDGE: In other words what you're saying is that you've been too intent on your main pursuits?

REITH: Yes.

MUGGERIDGE: And not sufficiently capable of putting them aside, relaxing, laughing, forgetting yourself.

REITH: Not nearly as much as I ought to have been. And that's why if I were sorry for anyone, it's for my wife, and to a lesser extent, but still a real extent, my son and daughter.

MUGGERIDGE: As we sit here tonight, in practically every home in this country this television thing will be switched on, and it will occupy for most of the people the evening hours. Anything to say about that at all?

REITH: It's a potential social menace of the first magnitude. Is that exaggeration?

MUGGERIDGE: Not in my eyes. Not in my eyes. Do you think there's been a moral – a lowering of moral standards in our society in recent years?

REITH: Yes, that's just what I was suggesting.

MUGGERIDGE: Do you think that the controllers of these mass communication media that have grown up in our time, all of them, could if they'd wished have checked this deterioration of moral standards?

REITH: You're talking about mass media generally?

MUGGERIDGE: Yes.

REITH: Yes, because they're not so minded, they haven't been so minded, or very few or them have.

MUGGERIDGE: And that's a condemnation of them or of our society or both?

REITH: Both.

MUGGERIDGE: This would seem to spell just decadence.

REITH: Is there no hope yet? Are we not permitted to hope? Has that been taken from us?

MUGGERIDGE: In other words the idea that our civilisation has run into a decline would be to you an alien thought?

REITH: Yes. I believe that there is rescue coming.

MUGGERIDGE: But from where?

REITH: I don't know. But I still believe it.

MUGGERIDGE: After all, civilisations in the past have declined, have disappeared. Why shouldn't ours?

REITH: You have the Roman Empire in mind, haven't you?

MUGGERIDGE: Yes. Let me read from your rectorial address:
'On that hard pagan world, disgust and secret loathing fell.
Deep weariness and sated lust made human life a hell.'
It's my conviction that that could happen to us in these islands.

REITH: And here is my comment and the burden, I suppose, of what I'm trying to say to you. For God's sake prevent it happening here.

Marriage
I think the interest of marriage and its pleasure is that it is perpetually having to be sorted out.

The Goat
Are you seriously suggesting on this programme that David Lloyd George was a monogamist?

Happiness

The sister-in-law of a friend of Dr Johnson was imprudent enough once to claim in his presence that she was happy. He pounced on her hard, remarking in a loud, emphatic voice that, if she was indeed the contented being she professed herself to be, then her life gave the lie to every research of humanity; for she was happy without health, without beauty, without money and without understanding. It was rough treatment, for which Johnson has been much criticised, though it should be remembered that he spoke as an eighteenth-century man, before our present preoccupation with happiness as an enduring condition of human life became prevalent. Actually I think I see his point.

There is something quite ridiculous and even indecent in an individual *claiming* to be happy. Still more a people or a nation making such a claim. The pursuit of happiness, included along with life and liberty in the American Declaration of Independence as an inalienable right, is without any question the most fatuous which could possibly be undertaken. This lamentable phrase 'the pursuit of happiness' (arrived at, incidentally, almost by accident on the spur of the moment because the Founding Fathers jibbed at the defence of property as an inalienable right) is responsible for a good part of the ills and miseries of the modern world.

To pursue happiness, individually or collectively, as a conscious aim is the surest way to miss it altogether; as is only too tragically evident in countries like Sweden and America where happiness has been most ardently pursued and where the material circumstances usually considered conducive to happiness have been most effectively constructed. The Gadarene swine were doubtless in pursuit of happiness when they hurled themselves to destruction over the cliff. Today the greater part of mankind, led by the technologically most advanced, are similarly bent, and if they persist will assuredly meet a similar fate. The pursuit of happiness, in any case, soon resolved itself into the pursuit of pleasure – something quite different. Pleasure is but a mirage of happiness – a false vision of shade and refreshment seen across parched sand.

Where, then, does happiness lie? In forgetfulness, not indulgence, of the self. In escape from sensual appetites, not in their satisfaction. We live in a dark, self-enclosed prison which is all we see or know if our glance is fixed ever downwards. To lift it upwards, becoming aware of the wide, luminous universe outside – this alone is happiness.

At its highest level such happiness is the ecstasy which mystics have inadequately described. At more humdrum levels it is human love; the delights and beauties of our dear earth, its colours and shapes and sounds; the enchantment of understanding and laughing, and all other exercise of such faculties as we possess; the marvel of the meaning of everything, fitfully glimpsed, inadequately expounded, but everpresent.

Such is happiness: not compressible into a pill; not translatable into a sensation; lost to whoever would grasp it to himself alone; not to be gorged out of a trough, or torn out of another's body, or paid into a bank, or driven along on an auto-route, or fired in gun-salutes, or discovered in the stratosphere. Existing, intangible, in every true response to life, and absent in every false one; propounded through the centuries in every noteworthy word and thought and deed; expressed in art and literature and music; in vast cathedrals and tiny melodies; in everything that is harmonious, and in the unending heroism of imperfect men reaching after perfection.

When Pastor Bonhoeffer was taken off by his Nazi guards to be executed, as I have read, his face was shining with happiness, to the point that even those poor clowns noted it. In that place of darkest evil he was the happiest man – he the executed. 'For you it is an end,' he told his executioners, 'but for me a beginning.' I find this an image of supreme happiness.

Failure

For myself I consider in all sincerity that I have been an abysmal failure. Over the last forty years I must have written, at a modest estimate, on an average some 5000 words a week, or, say, a quarter of a million words a year. The number I have spoken on radio or television I dare not contemplate. In all, ten million written words, of which so very, very few, if any, may be considered as having more than a momentary validity. Even the qualities I consider admirable – such as self-abnegation, loving kindness, unworldliness, spirituality – I have, but poorly, if at all, exemplified. I never heard of anyone of any account who believed he had been successful. Tolstoy, for instance, was so conscious of failure that, as he recounts in his autobiography, he found it necessary to hide away a rope that lay about in his study for fear of hanging himself with it. Shakespeare again (perhaps foreseeing the invention of television) wrote of himself with deep dissatisfaction:

> Tis true, alas, I have been here and there,
> and made myself a motley to the view. . . .

The reason is obvious. It is only possible to succeed at second-rate pursuits – like becoming a millionaire or a prime minister, winning a war, seducing beautiful women, flying through the stratosphere, or landing on the moon. First-rate pursuits – involving, as they must, trying to understand what life is about and trying to convey that understanding – inevitably result in a sense of failure. A Napoleon, a Churchill, a Roosevelt can feel themselves to be successful, but never a Socrates, a Pascal, a Blake. Understanding is for ever unattainable. Therein lies the inevitability of failure in embarking upon its quest, which is none the less the only one worthy of serious attention.

127

Of course I am well aware that there can be a sort of vanity and egotism in a sense of failure – for instance those Dostoevsky heroes who glory in their own abasement. It is dangerous to reason that, since all great men are conscious of being failures, therefore if I am conscious of being a failure I am a great man. One must watch out. All the same the Christian notion that the weak are strong and the foolish wise and the meek see God is sound enough. By the same token the successful are failures, and those who grasp in true humility the fallacy of success are, like the poor, blessed.

Prisons

Prisons have fostered far more supreme art and mystical insight than any Arts Council or Ministry of Culture.

Decisiveness

I think on the whole more harm is done by excessive decisiveness than by indecisiveness. Fortunately, we live in a country ruled by parliamentary government where indecision is the prevailing temper, and in that sense I think we can be thankful because we've had, during my lifetime, a number of very decisive gentlemen in charge of countries, namely Hitler, Mussolini, Stalin, and I think that I'd rather have, deplorable as it is, the bumbling indecisiveness of my parliamentary rulers. I myself, I'm happy to say, have rarely had to take any decisions that affect anybody else, except in writing leading articles, and that's the sort of ersatz, sham decisiveness in which you're sitting at a typewriter looking out of a window and you write marvellous sentences – like 'the people of this country will never for one moment countenance something or other' – and you know perfectly well they're going to countenance it with the utmost ease and satisfaction. The truth is that all the great questions of life, except those of ultimate faith, are questions that nobody but a fool will answer decisively.

Partition

A discussion in Any Questions? *with Douglas Hurd, then Political Secretary to the Prime Minister (Edward Heath) and now Minister of State at the Foreign Office, and Denis Healey, now Deputy Leader of the Labour Party.*

HURD: Partition is usually a device by which one generation stops its members from slaughtering each other. That's what happened in Ireland, in Palestine, in India and Pakistan. The question is whether the next generation can find a way of bringing the halves together without starting the slaughter over again. And I must say in none of those three cases which are actual at the moment, are we really in sight of that. I don't think you can blame the people who do the partition – they do it to stop people being killed.

MUGGERIDGE: Young Hurd, you've been indoctrinated by the current myth. To say that India and Pakistan were divided to stop slaughter – do you know how many people were slaughtered through the partition? Three million. These partitions are done because politicians can't think of a proper answer. Each of them leaves behind a hideous legacy to which in fact there's no answer. In the case of India and Pakistan, in order to get out quickly we allowed this ridiculous partition to take place which never had the remotest chance of working. In the Middle East, in order to get out of a mandate that we could no longer execute, we left a situation to which there is no solution, and similarly in Ireland. These dreadful situations are the harvest of devices adopted by politicians to evade solving a problem that confronts them.

HEALEY: Nobody who watched television night after night can think that the trouble in Northern Ireland is just a few wicked politicians. There is a real problem here. Ireland was partitioned after the First World War because a lot of Protestants in the North said they would fight unless they had a place to live. I think that partition at that time in practice was inevitable. I think the tragedy was that the line along which the partition was drawn deliberately included a large number of areas which were almost solid Catholic because the Protestants said they couldn't run a bit of Ireland unless they brought in Tyrone, Fermanagh and Derry and areas like that. But it's no good, Malcolm, imagining that ordinary people left alone without politicians will live together like the lion and the lamb.

MUGGERIDGE: But I didn't say that.

HEALEY: Partition in India happened because the Moslems – not the Moslem politicians – didn't want at that time to live with the Hindus, and I'm afraid there are many situations in which it's difficult to see an answer without partition. The only solution I've seen recently of a problem of this nature was where they exchanged populations between Greece and Turkey and there hasn't been that type of serious problem between them directly since then.

MUGGERIDGE: I must just point out that I wasn't saying that without politicians there'd be a solution. I said that these trouble spots were created by those in authority – namely politicians – not working out a proper solution. If you take the case of India and Pakistan, anybody who knew anything about it knew that this division was an intolerable arrangement. We should not have withdrawn to leave behind such a miserable state of affairs. Do you really think that anything you do now will reconcile the Irish to their country being divided? I don't.

HEALEY: I don't think you can in this, as in so many political problems, find anything you could call a solution. But I think you can hope to get through without the final disaster of a large-scale civil war, which, thank God, we haven't got so far. This is the real problem, whether the passions of ordinary human beings are still compatible with a peaceful solution. But all I say to you when you're slightly – I won't say offensive, but naughty – about politicians, do recognise that the problems that we nave to deal with are basically those created by the way in which ordinary people – who after all put them there – think and feel. As long as we remember that, we shan't make the mistake of believing that politicians can produce solutions simply by wanting to.

MUGGERIDGE: Now, listen, let's get this absolutely straight, Denis. My criticism of politicians arises from one thing only – that by virtue of their trade, they are the people who are responsible. It's their job. If you criticise me for things that I might write in newspapers, all this drivel, I would accept that as perfectly legitimate. Those three things that were drawn to our attention here were the work of politicians. I'm saying that it was shoddy work, that it was known at the time to many people to be shoddy work, and with the passage of years there comes the bill to pay.

HEALEY: I agree with you, Malcolm, if you'll accept that you write drivel, I'll agree that I sometimes make mistakes.

MUGGERIDGE: I accept – I accept it as an accolade, an accolade.

Political Appeal

In my opinion politicians are only bearable when they're slanging each other – as when the Earl of Sandwich said to Wilkes, 'You'll either die of the pox or come to the gallows,' to which Wilkes replied, 'That depends entirely on whether I embrace your Lordship's mistress or his principles.'

Looking back with Leonard Woolf

Remembering Virginia

Virginia Woolf wrote with great intensity and effort, reaching a kind of ecstasy of inspiration, and then correspondingly falling into the pit of despair. As we know from her journal, the strain of her writing taxed her precarious mental equilibrium, while stopping writing was liable to bring on bouts of depression. It was an appalling dilemma whose fluctuations in all their poignancy can be read as she recorded them day by day in her journal.

WOOLF (reading diary): This is an interesting piece because it's what she wrote about finishing *The Waves*. 'Here in the few minutes that remain I must record, heaven be praised, the end of *The Waves*. I wrote the words "oh death" fifteen minutes ago, having reeled across the last ten pages with some moments of such intensity and intoxication that I seemed only to stumble after my own voice, after some sort of speaker as when I was mad.'

MUGGERIDGE: Virginia's intermittent bouts of madness were the converse side of her genius – the sombre background against which her sparkle, her subtlety, her originality, her gaiety, her delight in people and companionship shone the more brightly. For you, Leonard, the alternations must have been an appalling strain: sitting over meals for hours coaxing her to eat, dreading a step in the night, hiding away the means of self-destruction.

WOOLF: She had alternations of what are called manic depression now. She could be very excited and exhilarated in a completely irrational way, talking in this state for days, until she became completely incoherent. I mean, the words meant nothing. Then she would fall into a coma, lasting for two days; and finally come to, and gradually recover.

MUGGERIDGE: It must have been absolutely hellish for you. But I have always been tremendously interested in the connection between her mental collapse and her writing. There must have been, of course, a connection.

WOOLF: I think it really is that her sort of genius was connected with her sort of madness and that you could see it in the way that her mind worked when she was perfectly sane. First of all in her own conversation she would suddenly do what I called 'leave the ground'. Suddenly she would begin telling one something quite ordinary, an incident that she'd seen in the street or something like that; and when her mind seemed to get completely off the ground she would give the most fascinating and amusing description of something fantastic, quite unlike anything that anyone other than herself would have thought of, which would last for about five or ten minutes.

MUGGERIDGE: Of course that is what is meant by inspiration. We have all felt it to a minute degree that one is racing after some meaning that is ahead of us.

WOOLF: Yes. And not only that. I think that very rarely, when one is writing, suddenly a thought or phrase comes into one's mind which seems to be out of one's control; that one hadn't thought of it oneself. And I think that, with people who are inclined to be mad and also inclined to be geniuses, that goes on with much greater intensity.

MUGGERIDGE: Blake was an example.

WOOLF: Yes.

MUGGERIDGE: I mean he barely understood himself. But then, Leonard, how did it happen that this ecstasy was combined with this black despair, and led her in the end to take her own life?

WOOLF: I think it was an exaggeration of what everyone feels. You get out of bed one day on the wrong side and you're miserable, and the next day you get out of bed in the morning, and you're exhilarated. And if you're exhilarated, it's ten to one that you will be depressed before the evening. My nurse always used to say that there'll be tears before the evening if I was very excited. You see, I think that the exhilaration of her inspiration, of her writing, was followed by a depression. Both were not really under her control and much more violent than ordinary people's. Her depression would become so great that she would think life was no longer worth living.

MUGGERIDGE: And end it.

WOOLF: And end it.

MUGGERIDGE: What do you feel about suicide?

WOOLF: I think it's a lamentable thing as it happens, but I think if life isn't worth living one ought to commit suicide. I can't feel that I would, but I've got no objection to other people doing it if they want to.

MUGGERIDGE: You don't feel that society should set its face against it?

WOOLF: No.

MUGGERIDGE: Which of course has been the Christian attitude, hasn't it? You don't approve of that?

WOOLF: No, I think it's absurd. Don't you?

MUGGERIDGE: Well, I don't actually, no, because I think that you've got to – that society must discourage people from doing this.

WOOLF: Yes, but it's absurd. If you commit suicide, you're done for, you can't be punished. You're only punished for not succeeding in committing suicide.

MUGGERIDGE: I agree that it's illogical, but it still remains clear to me that it is absolutely terrible that such a thing should happen.

WOOLF: Oh, it's appalling – and also the process. If one had seen it, as I did, seen it with one's own eyes. It's only if there's been an appalling amount of mental torture such as she went through when she felt that she was going mad and that she couldn't control her thoughts, it was only when she got to that stage that she committed suicide, and of course the process of getting to that stage was absolutely appalling to – to watch.

MUGGERIDGE: Agony, I should think. But you must have been aware all the time that this was liable to happen.

WOOLF: Oh yes. As soon as I realised what it was, of course, it was what one had to guard against. Not that at any moment she would have committed suicide, because that wasn't the case. The process by which anyone with that mental disease, because it really is a disease, reaches the suicide stage is quite a long process. At times she would be perfectly all right and walk out into the garden without any danger of committing suicide. It was only after one of these long attacks in which she got more and more depressed and couldn't sleep or write, or work or see people, then she felt that she would never recover and would try to commit suicide.

MUGGERIDGE: Was it the price she paid for producing her books?

WOOLF: I think it was really.

Animals

I feel an instinctive loathing of this idea that animals must be treated with complete contempt in order that they may serve men. Don't misunderstand me. The position that I'm stating, as I am well aware, is incapable of a logical application. I'm only putting in a proviso that I notice in the society in which I live, as I get older, a sort of attitude towards animals that they are purely for our food, purely to serve our interests, and that we can treat them as we like. And I think that this will be very dangerous because ultimately it will rebound against human beings. Blake said, 'A robin redbreast in a cage puts high heaven in a rage.' Marvellous. Marvellous couplet. Profoundly true. A robin redbreast in a cage puts high heaven in a rage. I agree.

With Leonard Woolf, in Sussex, 1967.

With Lord Reith at Glasgow University, 1967.

Malcolm Muggeridge as The Gryphon *in Jonathan Miller's television production of* Alice In Wonderland.

'Sir John Gielgud as the Mock Turtle and myself as the Gryphon found ourselves prancing along the seashore near Hastings in the Lobster Quadrille without any specific directives. For me it was like dancing with some immensely experienced and accomplished partner whose expertise carries one along. Yet over and above that there was the situation as set up by Jonathan Miller – two old fellows with their preposterous melancholy and flippancy under the cool disdainful gaze of a child.'

Let Me Speak. *Among the groups of young people with something emphatic to say who appeared on this programme were these Anarchists (August 1964).*

Pilgrim's Progress

A discussion with Aneurin Bevan

MUGGERIDGE: I read *Pilgrim's Progress* again the other day, and I was enormously struck by how it stands up. What a perfect image it is of human life.

BEVAN: Well, Mr Muggeridge, I'm afraid I don't agree with that. You see, it's all so simple. You always know that Faithful is going to be faithful. You always know that Mr Greatheart is never going to give in; and life's much more complex than that.

MUGGERIDGE: Well, don't forget the case of Christian himself, Mr Bevan. After all he changes all right and his character develops. He is led astray and then he finds the way again, and he listens to false counsel and then comes to realise it's false.

BEVAN: Yes, he does; but then you see we read the names. One is called Fearful, the other is called Ignorance. There's no suspense in the book, there's no tension. It's not epic drama, it's melodrama, precisely because of that fact.

MUGGERIDGE: I wouldn't agree with that at all because one does have the feeling of anxiety. Is he going to make it? Is he going to get to the end? Just as one does if one reads a play like *Macbeth* for the thirtieth time. One knows perfectly well that Duncan is going to be murdered, and at the same time anxiety is there.

BEVAN: Ah, but in the case of *Macbeth* you have a drama. In the case of *Macbeth* you have conflicting forces inside people as well as outside people. The great soliloquy of Lady Macbeth is itself evidence of remorse, of tension, of apprehension of the future, but it's inside her. What Bunyan has done is personify the qualities of men in different personalities.

MUGGERIDGE: I quite agree that he intended an allegory; but

the miracle of *Pilgrim's Progress* is that it turned into the first novel in the English language.

BEVAN: It may be the first novel, but it is not, in terms of the modern scene, sufficiently illuminating or rewarding.

MUGGERIDGE: I think that's the great point of difference between you and me. You think that the modern scene has invalidated *Pilgrim's Progress* and I think that it remains *as* valid in the modern scene and indeed in any conceivable human scene.

BEVAN: It never was any good because in the first place it was too obvious, in the second place it simplifies life to the point where it is of no assistance to anyone, and in the third place it becomes exceedingly dull.

MUGGERIDGE: I don't agree with that at all. To me it's fascinating, and it's fascinating because I get a living sense of human beings.

BEVAN: I'm bound to say that if Mr Muggeridge can find *Pilgrim's Progress* fascinating he's a very easy man to write for.

MUGGERIDGE: I'm not alone. This book has been found fascinating by millions of people, literally millions of people.

BEVAN: I wonder. It's a sort of thing that you have as part of your furniture. I expect you can visit many homes and you see *Pilgrim's Progress* there with uncut leaves.

MUGGERIDGE: Well, my children loved reading it, I can assure you of that, and furthermore it's been translated into every language. Now I can't believe that all that would have been undertaken merely, as Mr Bevan suggests, in order to have a respectable book to put on a shelf. That's beyond my powers of imagination.

BEVAN: Now may I make another point about *Pilgrim's Progress* which in fact I think is very rarely made. I think Bunyan himself was not writing primarily a religious tract. He was writing a political tract. He says at the beginning, 'A man clothed with rags, standing in a certain place, a book in his hand, and a great burden upon his back.' Well, of course that burden is said to be sin, but over and over again it is obviously the burden of poverty of which he is speaking. He is a poor man fighting against established institutions.

MUGGERIDGE: I was waiting for this to happen. You see we're moving on. Bunyan has got to be a Bevanite. That's the truth of it.

BEVAN: Wouldn't he – wouldn't he be now if he were alive?

MUGGERIDGE: I once looked up his biography and the curious thing about him is that it's not even by any means certain that he was on the Parliamentary side in the Civil War. I doubt whether Mr Bevan would have been.

BEVAN: . . . malevolence, Mr Muggeridge.

MUGGERIDGE: I love this book because it transcends the things you've mentioned. I quite agree that Bunyan was poor; I quite agree that he went to prison; I quite agree that he was anguished that people should be in poverty; but I don't believe that the burden that he carried on his back was his burden of poverty, and I don't believe that his beautiful raiment, when he lost his rags, was provided by the Ministry of Health.

BEVAN: Why do you think he was put in prison?

MUGGERIDGE: He was put in prison because he was naturally, as all good men are, a nonconformist.

BEVAN: No, no, no. He was put in prison because people of his way of thinking were regarded as rebels. He uses the language of levellers. It's a protest; and if you notice, when he comes to certain cities he is taken secretly to one of his friends who is known to the others. There is a conspiratorial quality about the book which is only credible when you consider it as a political pamphlet, shared by a number of people who are conspiring against established institutions.

MUGGERIDGE: I wouldn't deny at all that from the point of view of the State he was subversive. I'm saying, though, that he was subversive in the sense that all sound human beings are subversive. He was subversive because of his own conscience and not because of the political philosophy. What the State asked Bunyan to do under the King was to stop preaching.

BEVAN: I didn't say it was a political philosophy and I admit at once that the book does develop a momentum as a religious tract, but I think that Bunyan intended it to be read differently. Otherwise, why say in his address to the readers 'Do not play with the outside of my dream'?

MUGGERIDGE: All holy men are subversive. St Augustine was a subversive.

BEVAN: Quite frequently in that period, Mr Muggeridge, as you know, people had to write pamphlets of social progress in a religious guise.

MUGGERIDGE: Of course.

BEVAN: They had to do it. There was a double meaning. . . .

MUGGERIDGE: Yes, but I do not think that in that beautiful phrase that you've quoted, he meant 'Don't think this is really about God and about being good, it's actually about the National Health Service'.

BEVAN: Let me read some more in order to show how Christian comes back over and over again to the economic problems of the day. Mr Worldly-Wiseman says: 'Hear me, I am older than thou. Thou art like to meet in the way thou goest wearisomeness, painfulness, hunger, perils, nakedness, swords lie in dragon's darkness' and so on, and Christian replies, 'Why sir, this burden upon my back is more terrible to me than all these things which you have mentioned,' and then Worldly-Wiseman repeats, 'It has happened unto other weak men, whom, meddling with things too high for them, do suddenly fall into thy distractions.'

MUGGERIDGE: But, Mr Bevan, the meaning of that is as clear as day, and it's the exact opposite of what you're saying.

BEVAN: And it's precisely because, if that is what you mean by the meaning of the book, it's so obviously dull.

MUGGERIDGE: If Mr Bevan regards it as a tract on social progress I would agree with him entirely; it's a second-rate one. But to me it is an exquisite image of a human being struggling with the difficulties of life and the confusion of moral values.

BEVAN: But it does not move me, because I cannot conceivably imagine in terms of our knowledge of men and women today how anybody can be condemned to hell fire, for example. I don't believe that people who sin sometimes, because they can't help it, or because they've got the wrong parents, are necessarily going to be condemned to eternal damnation.

MUGGERIDGE: Well I think that's a 'red herring'. The point really is Christian's journey. The day-by-day struggle. The Hill difficulty, the Slough of Despond, the Delectable Mountains. All those things are exquisitely described.

BEVAN: But then his reward is eternal glory.

MUGGERIDGE: But that's just an image.

BEVAN: I cannot sympathise with individuals who are either going to earn eternal glory, or who are condemned to horrible torment for things over which they can have no control at all.

MUGGERIDGE: Because an imagery becomes obsolete, it's validity doesn't become obsolete, that's the point.

BEVAN: I still maintain he was in fact speaking about his own people. When they read him, when they read that wonderful direct description of a man with a burden on his back, they read it because they saw in it what they wanted to see, which was a protest against the actual conditions of their lives.

The Labour Party
In the Labour Party there's always been an extra element of comedy in that the people who are ostensibly leading it have very little power, and the people who are in the wings have a great deal of power. I remember realising this at a party conference I had to cover. Gaitskell was making a very long speech about Labour Party policy, and sitting near him was a rather nice trade union leader, the late Arthur Deakin. He had several million votes in his pocket, which is calculated to give anyone a slight edge, isn't it? Well, Gaitskell was going on and on. Suddenly it grew too much for Deakin, who shouted out in a quite audible voice: 'Shut your gob!' I thought to myself, 'Heaven be praised, at last the reality of this conference has been made manifest.'

Alice in Wonderland

The Gryphon speaks

Jonathan Miller's production is based on the situation of a real little girl confronted with the absurd grown-up world of unreality which she will have to enter when, shortly, she reaches puberty. He sees Lewis Carroll's *Alice* as one more sick Victorian cry in the night against the monstrous encroachment of adolescence on the purity and innocence of childhood. Project it a little further and you get to Barrie and *Peter Pan*, a little further still and you get to Nabokov and *Lolita*. For Barrie the first drops of menstrual blood were all too terribly an intimation of mortality, the first leaden raindrops before a violent thunderstorm.

The reference to *Lolita* may seem far-fetched, but not after looking through the Rev. Charles Dodgson's collection of photographs, a selection of which were published in 1949, edited with an interesting introduction by Mr Helmut Gern-sheim. The photographs are nearly all of little girls in various conditions of undress; 'I wish,' Dodgson wrote to the *Punch* artist Harry Furniss, 'I dared dispense with *all* costume. Naked children are so perfectly pure and lovely; but Mrs Grundy would be furious – it would never do.' Children for him meant little girls – 'I confess I do *not* admire naked boys. They always seem to me to need clothes – whereas one hardly sees why the lovely forms of girls should ever be covered up.' Humbert Humbert would have understood perfectly. Sometimes parents did not object, and then Mrs Grundy could be ignored, though 'if I had the loveliest child in the world, to draw or photograph, and found she had a modest shrinking (however slight, and however easily over-come) from being taken nude, I should feel it was a solemn duty owed to God to drop the request *altogether*.'

It is highly characteristic of our time that Miller's transfer-ence of *Alice's Adventures in Wonderland* from the sick mind of Lewis Carroll to the sane mind of Alice herself should seem to imply the vicious travesty of an enchanting children's tale. *Alice* might conceivably bore juvenile viewers of all ages, it could not possibly shock them. This apart from any consid-eration as to whether children reared on *Batman* and occa-sional glimpses of adult favourites like *Peyton Place* and *The Man from UNCLE* are in fact shockable at all. *Alice* has long been part of contemporary folklore, and Miller's version, giving it a new, significant twist, necessarily becomes a piece of social history.

Secretaries

I've suffered a great deal from secretaries in my life; I'm practically a sort of martyr to secretaries. If there was a special kind of disease, like housemaid's knee, if you could have secretary's thumb, I would have it.

Tailor and Cutter

A sartorial dispute

MUGGERIDGE: I've got here tonight Mr John Taylor, who's the editor of the *Tailor and Cutter*, a very eminent journal, supreme in its field, and I'm going to ask him, if he'd be so kind, without being unduly insulting, to comment on my appearance.

TAYLOR: Well, as long as you have no solicitors secreted about you, Mr Muggeridge, I would say that the thing that mainly worries me about you is a sort of greyness that you present –

MUGGERIDGE: It's drab you think?

TAYLOR: No, not necessarily, but rather unimaginative – the grey shirt, the grey tie, the grey suit –

MUGGERIDGE: Shabby?

TAYLOR: No, no, no, but coupled with the grey hair and the grey eyebrows it's rather a formidable experience you know. The jacket is very nice, it's short, which of course is a fashionable thing, but I rather feel that you've had that one long enough for the fashion to come round again –

MUGGERIDGE: Mr Taylor, you're dead right – but that was no question of a feeling for fashion, it was just simple poverty.

TAYLOR: Of course when we get . . . may I?

MUGGERIDGE: Oh do, take anything off you like – do you want me to take my trousers off?

TAYLOR: No – no – no, not at the moment. I would say the trousers, incidentally, are rather baggy and they look a – your braces haven't broken, have they, Mr Muggeridge?

MUGGERIDGE: No, I don't think so. The whole thing is holding up, I'm glad to say.

TAYLOR: They could do without the turn-up, I think. But again, getting back to this grey thing – grey – grey – grey – grey – grey – and suddenly brown boots and blue socks.

MUGGERIDGE: Not boots, old boy, shoes.

TAYLOR: And blue socks – don't you think this is –

MUGGERIDGE: Is it a little indelicate?

TAYLOR: I think so – yes.

MUGGERIDGE: Of course I'm no expert on this matter, but I would awfully like to look at your very elegant get-up. Now this particular double-breasted waistcoat – is that a fashionable thing?

TAYLOR: Well that helps with the new fashion, the padded stomach –

MUGGERIDGE: Now this tie of yours –

TAYLOR: – you don't like that?

MUGGERIDGE: Well, I wouldn't say I don't like it, I just think it's a tiny bit fanciful.

TAYLOR: Well, of course I'm a fanciful person.

MUGGERIDGE: And what about this little flower here?

TAYLOR: Well that is a compliment to you, Mr Muggeridge – I must say that I'm rather surprised you didn't return this compliment.

MUGGERIDGE: And what about these trousers of yours – they seem a bit spidery, you know.

TAYLOR: Spidery?

MUGGERIDGE: Mmm.

TAYLOR: Well no – you see, there's a fine strong leg within it to sustain –

MUGGERIDGE: I'm sure of that – yes.

TAYLOR: – that's probably why you have to build yours out a little wider –

MUGGERIDGE: You mean to cover these old lean shanks?

TAYLOR: That could be it –

MUGGERIDGE: And what about these shoes? – I think they're rather like slippers.

TAYLOR: Slippers?

MUGGERIDGE: You couldn't walk out in those shoes, could you?

TAYLOR: I can keep them on – yes –

MUGGERIDGE: And hold them on?

TAYLOR: I still have my arches, of course.

MUGGERIDGE: You have your arches. Now do you, as a matter of fact, keep your socks up with a suspender or by will power?

TAYLOR: Well I actually hook them over my leg muscle – that would be another problem for you, wouldn't it?

MUGGERIDGE: Could we just take a peep at the lower leg – there's nothing indelicate –

TAYLOR: Yes indeed –

MUGGERIDGE: Very good indeed. But isn't that a tiny bit chilly?

TAYLOR: No – no – no – I'm a warm-blooded person.

MUGGERIDGE: Mr Taylor, long combinations do not –

TAYLOR: Oh, never at all –

MUGGERIDGE: – play any role in your life at all?

TAYLOR: You don't wear them at all, do you, Mr Muggeridge?

MUGGERIDGE: Well I prefer not to go into that, but I was just asking you, that you don't in fact do anything of that sort?

TAYLOR: No, nothing of that sort.

MUGGERIDGE: Mr Taylor, do you regard fashion for men as a very edifying thing?

TAYLOR: Oh I certainly do. I mean, what do you expect me to say? Of course I do, my whole life depends upon it.

The English Cardinal

A personal view of
John Carmel Heenan, Archbishop of Westminster

In back numbers of *Punch* funny bishops and curates abound. Similarly in novels of clerical life, like Trollope's *Barchester Towers*. But there are no funny Cardinals. The traditional English scene just doesn't seem to accommodate them. Yet Cardinals indubitably exist. Witness John Carmel Heenan, our only extant specimen; Archbishop of Westminster, and head of the Roman Catholic Church in England; the English Cardinal.

MUGGERIDGE: I always feel that almost the only reason that I'd like to become a Cardinal would be to be waited on by nuns.

CARDINAL: I think you'd make a very good Cardinal as a matter of fact.

MUGGERIDGE: I doubt it strongly. Not a Cardinal, perhaps a bishop.

CARDINAL: Well, you've got to start somewhere.

MUGGERIDGE: I always like lunching on Fridays because we don't have meat.

CARDINAL: You're not getting any fish, by the way, you're getting an omelette.

MUGGERIDGE: No, no, it's very nice. This would be part of the Catholic life that I would find least difficult. I suppose it dates from a time when eating meat was a tremendously important thing.

CARDINAL: Well, you know what they say. They say that it was an example of the Jewish instinct of the twelve Apostles; they were all fishermen, and they decided that if they made a rule about fish on Fridays, it would be good business. But I don't think that's a theological doctrine.

MUGGERIDGE: How powerful is a Cardinal today?

CARDINAL: How powerful? It really depends on what you mean by power.

MUGGERIDGE: But aren't you the boss of the bishops?

CARDINAL: The boss of the bishops? No, the Pope is.

MUGGERIDGE: But he's your boss?

CARDINAL: The Pope is my boss, but he's also the boss of all the bishops. The Pope deals directly with the bishops, not through me necessarily.

MUGGERIDGE: He can go over your head as it were?

CARDINAL: Well, yes. I wouldn't think of it in that way.

MUGGERIDGE: No. But the thing is that of course the Church does indulge in the sort of magnificence and outward show which one associates with worldly power.

CARDINAL: When you're taking part in rituals, as I do very often, it is burdensome rather than self-glorifying.

MUGGERIDGE: You mean you personally don't like it too much.

CARDINAL: Well, no, and also you've got to wear the robes. The same as the poor Queen when she wears the crown and the royal robes. I'm sure she's most uncomfortable but nevertheless she knows that by doing this she gives a certain satisfaction to her people.

MUGGERIDGE: To me, at any rate, such emulation of the trappings of earthly authority would seem to have a certain danger.

CARDINAL: This outward panoply and foolishness that you are thinking of, this has its uses, because even sticking a chain round a man's neck and calling him mayor of Wigan – I don't mean that with any disrespect to Wigan, of course – but putting a chain round a man's neck marks him out as chief citizen. If he's not a fool he doesn't really think he's the brightest and best and most intelligent man in that particular town. Nevertheless, that chain of office shows him to be what he is; it's a sign – a badge of his office. Incidentally, I've got a chain on too, with a Cross, and I always envy a Mayor his chain, because at the end of the year he can just take it off and go off on his own, but this thing will be with me until I'm in the coffin in the Cathedral. . . .

Cardinal Heenan's own origin and background – Irish extraction, lower middle class – have been no impediment to his elevation to his present eminence. Indeed, these antecedents become the Roman Catholic Church in England better than, say, a seat in the House of Lords. A large proportion of the English Roman Catholic Church's four million or so members are Irish, or of Irish extraction. There is a small admixture of aristocrats from the old English Catholic families and a few notable intellectual camp followers. But in the main English Roman Catholics tend to be artisans and poor. This may partly account for the continuing appeal of a glittering liturgy and ceremonial: the poor need dreams of magnificence to compensate for the bareness of their lives. Only Quakers are rich enough to worship austerely.

MUGGERIDGE: How about your role as proselytiser?

CARDINAL: I loathe that word.

MUGGERIDGE: Presumably you want more people to become Roman Catholics?

CARDINAL: Yes. I want everybody to.

MUGGERIDGE: Therefore you are a sort of missionary.

CARDINAL: I object to the word proselytiser because it sounds like something very underhand, some poison, some snaky movement by which you're trying to drag people from the truth and indoctrinate them. . . . No, you wouldn't call Christ a proselytiser; a preacher perhaps. We call the Apostles –

MUGGERIDGE: Evangelists.

CARDINAL: Evangelists, men who have the message, which they believe to be true, and want to spread it everywhere. Now there's nothing strange about that, because even if you happened to have discovered a cough cure and it really works, and you take this thing, this drug or injection, all winter, and never have a cold, you know well that you cannot stop telling your friends about it. If you're a good man and you possess a good thing, you want to share it. There's an old philosophical saying, *Bonum est diffusivum sui*. You'll know this, of course, but for the sake of my colleagues on the bench I will translate. It means that goodness diffuses itself, spreads itself, it can't help it, just as heat can't help expanding, warmth glows. In this kind of way a person who possesses the faith wants to spread it, wants his warmth to go out to others. Now that's no problem to me. Is it a problem to you?

MUGGERIDGE: No, not a problem at all.

CARDINAL: But this is what you've got to remember. Although we don't use the word because it's an offensive kind of word to use, this country's full of pagans, this country's full of people who know as little about God as the so-called heathens that you mentioned.

MUGGERIDGE: Since you would hold that your Church in certain respects has the message uniquely, you would presumably wish good Anglicans also to join it.

CARDINAL: Well naturally; after all this country was once a completely Catholic country, as you know. It would be lovely if once again it could be a completely Catholic country, from my point of view. Whereas, as you know, others would say, 'Oh no, just a moment, it was once a Catholic country, but then the corruption of Rome spread, and it had to be cured by a complete revival and renewal, and then the old Catholic faith was restored and Romanism dissipated.' That's another point of view – not, as it happens, mine.

MUGGERIDGE: I didn't think it was. Anyway, the point is that presumably, in so far as you would in the long run hope to bring back the Anglican church into the fold, into the Roman Catholic fold, that would mean that you were a missionary in relation to them also; that even the Archbishop of Canterbury, say, is a target.

CARDINAL: Well, target is hardly the word.

MUGGERIDGE: How do you get along with him, incidentally?

CARDINAL: He's a very great friend of mine; I'm very fond of him, and of his wife too.

MUGGERIDGE: Do you argue with him when you're there?

CARDINAL: I don't think we argue in the sense of have controversy. It's clear that as the Chief Bishop of the Church, the Anglican Church in this country and throughout the world, it's hardly likely that when I go to Lambeth I would go with a whole bundle of tracts in my pocket and say, 'Look, I must explain to you about Papal infallibility'. Of course not. Our conversation's on a very different kind of level, and I don't think he ever seriously tries to persuade me of the errors of Rome or offer me a job as his assistant or auxiliary bishop in Canterbury. No, we don't do that. But if you ask me, I don't want to appear in any way insincere. I do agree that my greatest desire would be to have all Englishmen Catholics again.

MUGGERIDGE: And those little churches and cathedrals that used to be Catholic – all their bells would be ringing.

In Rome, of course, bells of Catholic churches have been ringing longer and more loudly than anywhere else. In Rome, the centre of Christianity since its beginning some 2000 years ago, Cardinal Heenan's position is both magnified and reduced – magnified because he is part of a universal church rather than head of a minority communion – reduced because he is one Cardinal among many instead of the unique specimen. There are many Cardinals but only one Pope.

The Ecumenical Council, somewhat impulsively called by Pope Paul's predecessor, Pope John, has been inescapably confronted with some of the most explosive dilemmas of our time. The twentieth century, it would seem, has broken into one of the last and most powerful citadels holding out against its incursions. Yet, in'the eyes of an outsider like myself, this seems more of a lavishly mounted spectacular than a solemn act of worship.

These Cardinals and Bishops – such extraordinary and diverse old faces! Such a variety of races and nationalities! These are the appointed custodians of the rock on which, in their estimation, the whole structure of Christendom has been founded. None more so than Cardinal Heenan. He has been educated, brought up, trained for that very purpose. He looks round on a world full of doubt and uncertainty and rejoices the more in his own certainties. Then the scene changes, the authority that's everything seems to be wavering. The rock itself is shaken. Basic concepts like original sin lose their fine definition. Is it possible that concupiscence, fortified by the birth pill, is after all permissible? Can it be Lady Chatterley approaching the altar rails?

Rome is for Cardinal Heenan almost as much home territory as London or Liverpool. He was a student at the English College and the Georgian University here. Yet I should not say myself that he seems more at home than he does in St James's Park. All unusual men, I have noticed, give an

impression of being strangers in a strange land; only medioc-
rities easily acclimatise themselves to their mortality. Yet it
is, of course, impossible really to get inside someone else's
skin, least of all a demolition man inside a custodian's. Yet
one can, without presumption, sense in Cardinal Heenan the
strain and even the anguish of seeing cherished beliefs under
attack. Not just from without – that's taken for granted,
that's what martyrdom, which he has been taught to believe
a Christian's highest destiny, is about – but from within the
Church itself.

CARDINAL: You've got to be quite mature before you realise
what being a priest involves, particularly in the question of
celibacy, giving up the right to a family and so on, and it's at
that time, I think, that the crisis comes with most people.
These young men realise, they might be 20, 19, 21, anything,
but they'll be quite mature and they will then say, 'Now, for
the first time I realise that this really does mean a lonely life'.
You're not feeling miserable because you're alone, but you're
a man apart.

The relationship between a Catholic priest and his people is
something you've got to experience to understand, they call
me Father and that's a term of tremendous affection. Now
that Fatherhood I find enormously attractive and uplifting,
but the shouting and the kissing, that means very little
indeed.

MUGGERIDGE: What do people want from their religion?

CARDINAL: It's the unchanging teaching of the Church which
answers the deepest appeal, I think, in the heart of the people.

MUGGERIDGE: What is that unchanging teaching, in a word?

CARDINAL: In a word, if you want *a* word – authority.

MUGGERIDGE: Authority, whose authority?

CARDINAL: The authority of the Church, made known
through the Pope and through the Council.

MUGGERIDGE: Contrasting with that, when you're standing at
the altar . . . ?

CARDINAL: Now that's quite different. When I'm standing at

the altar, I am there representing Christ. When I offer the Mass, I don't say, 'This is the Body of Christ,' I say, 'This is my Body,' because I, John Heenan, don't exist. That's why the vestments are there to disguise my personality. I am standing there as a mediator, as one representing Christ. That's quite different; there I am the Church, so to speak.

MUGGERIDGE: This is the difficult thing to understand.

CARDINAL: Of course, of course.

MUGGERIDGE: I mean, how do you feel, when you're doing it?

CARDINAL: Well, I've been a priest for thirty-five years, and I've offered Mass every day.

MUGGERIDGE: For thirty-five years.

CARDINAL: Yes, and sometimes more than once a day. Now, there's an old saying, an old Latin saw – *Ab assuetis non fit passio* – a thing you're used to doesn't affect you, and so, obviously, I don't feel emotionally now as I did the day I put on vestments for the first time, and offered my first Mass as a young priest. I don't feel the same but perhaps I treasure the Mass even more; the Mass means more to me now after thirty-five years of celebration daily, than it did then. But how to describe that and how to show that that should be so is very difficult.

MUGGERIDGE: Does it add to your worries when you think that by and large people are falling away from the Christian religion?

CARDINAL: Of course, of course. I don't use the word worry, because I don't worry about these things. It's God's business you know. If they're falling away from religion, they're falling away from Him.

MUGGERIDGE: But you wouldn't feel that it's because you're being inadequate?

CARDINAL: Yes, yes.

MUGGERIDGE: Do you, when you wake up in the night, think that . . .

CARDINAL: How do you know I wake up in the night?

MUGGERIDGE: I'm sure you're a fellow-insomniac. I can spot them. When you wake up, would it be a thing that would worry you to think to yourself, 'Well, are we really making a great mistake?'

CARDINAL: No, I don't. On this, no. I have no doubts whatever.

MUGGERIDGE: You would regard yourself as being a person who held, on the whole, for tradition?

CARDINAL: Well yes, I would say that every Catholic really at heart values the tradition. You can't be a Catholic without holding for tradition. We're the one thing in a changing world that's solid. We're the thing that people can reach for.

MUGGERIDGE: But you are going to go on being as solid as you have been?

CARDINAL: I hope so. Of course we are. Rome is the centre of Christianity. This place is still the centre, and that's not because of that material building. Because, you see, this city of Rome could be taken over by the communists tomorrow, or next year. But even if materially we abandoned Rome, the spiritual centre of the Church is the Pope, the Vicar of Christ, and, as you know, there have been Popes that have never seen Rome. At one time there were no less than three people claiming to be the Pope. There was vice in this Vatican. This was a centre of vice from time to time, the Borgia Popes and so on, and therefore we are sometimes inclined to think that this was the most wicked of all ages, but in fact, in many ways, it's the best of all ages. And you asked some time ago where I stood, and was I against progress. The answer is no. But obviously when you get people emotionally charged and determined to broaden the view, there are going to be excesses, they're going to exaggerate, they're going to get it wrong, and some of us have got to stand quite firm and say, 'Yes, I love this wide open view, but we mustn't for a moment forget truth, we mustn't pretend that truth doesn't matter.'

I put to myself these questions about Cardinal Heenan: A hard man? I shouldn't say so; severe, perhaps, though even that more in outward appearance than inward temperament. Severe certainly with himself. An ambitious man? Yes, but only in the sense of wanting to fulfil to the uttermost his priestly functions. An intolerant man? Undoubtedly with, for instance, the uncertainties and hesitancies of intellectuals. A narrow man? In a way, yes. An evangelist through and through, wrapped up in pastoral duties and responsibilities, wholly concerned with propagating the Faith, of which he has a clear, but possibly over-simplified version. A good man? Who can tell? Lacking some elements of greatness, like a wide vision and the imaginative gifts to project it, but possessing others, like clarity, sincerity and an all-absorbing passion to carry out God's will; underneath the surface confidence, a touching and true humility which I have glimpsed from time to time. A great and formidable priest, anyway, for the mid-twentieth century.

The Establishment

Every time I see the Archbishop of Canterbury on the screen I am conscious that – to adapt a famous saying of Voltaire – if he did not exist it would be impossible to invent him. Efforts to ridicule those set in authority over us are constantly frustrated by their own intrinsic ridiculousness. I mean, who can hope to improve on the original of, say, a George Brown or a Ted Heath? Their native absurdity exceeds by far the wildest and most fantastic inventions. These public figures are snatching the bread out of the mouths of professional entertainers just by being themselves. Why shouldn't they have to join Equity and submit their scripts to the Lord Chamberlain like everyone else? Why, for that matter, shouldn't they come on The Late Show *and save John Bird the trouble of impersonating them? Here an awesome thought strikes me. Perhaps they do.*

The Established Church

The identification of a church and a state is about as farcical as a vegetarian joining the Butcher's Union.

The Ten Commandments

My own view of the Ten Commandments is very like that of an Anglican Bishop who once said, and I think it's very typical of the whole Anglican Church, that they are like an examination paper – eight only to be attempted.

Veteran Humorist

A conversation with P. G. Wodehouse

Hilaire Belloc called him the greatest prose writer of our time. Evelyn Waugh acknowledged him as a master. In his eighties P. G. Wodehouse is still hard at it. Bertie Wooster and his gentleman's gentleman, Jeeves, take their place along with Don Quixote and Sancho Panza. Wodehouse lives now in seclusion in one of the remoter parts of Long Island some eighty miles from New York. He's become an American. Some broadcasts that he inadvertently delivered in Berlin during the War damaged his reputation for a time among his fellow countrymen without, however, diminishing the number of Wodehouse addicts or the pleasures of their addiction.

MUGGERIDGE: Plummy, when were you last in England?

WODEHOUSE: Well, I actually came over for one day to see a cricket match in 1939, but apart from that I haven't been over since 1934.

MUGGERIDGE: Do you have a picture of England as it is now?

WODEHOUSE: Well I wonder, has it altered? Of course I get all the English papers. It doesn't sound as if it has altered so tremendously.

MUGGERIDGE: I don't know whether the old Drones Club would be quite as flourishing.

WODEHOUSE: No, I suppose everybody's got a job now.

MUGGERIDGE: The great thing about Bertie Wooster, as I recall, is that he never had anything particular to do, did he?

WODEHOUSE: Oh no, Bertie never did, no, he didn't do a stroke.

MUGGERIDGE: I think now he'd have to get a job in advertising or something, don't you think so?

160

WODEHOUSE: He'd have to get a job I think, oh yes.

MUGGERIDGE: Of course, in Jeeves you have created the most famous butler in the history of the world. Among your own acquaintances have you known many butlers?

WODEHOUSE: Well, I've had a lot of butlers. I must say they were never anything like Jeeves.

MUGGERIDGE: What were your butlers like?

WODEHOUSE: Well, one of them – I forget which one it was, during the twenties – was jugged for robbery with violence, and he got about three years.

MUGGERIDGE: Jeeves has never been such a fool as to let himself be caught.

WODEHOUSE: No, Jeeves never would.

MUGGERIDGE: What do you feel about humorous writing today?

WODEHOUSE: It's rather depressing the way humour has died out. I mean, all the humour you get nowadays seems to be that vicious humour, you know; Lennie Bruce sort of stuff.

MUGGERIDGE: Anyway your books go on selling, don't they?

WODEHOUSE: The extraordinary thing is foreign countries seem to like them. The Swedes have always been very faithful.

MUGGERIDGE: Wodehouse standbys.

WODEHOUSE: But Italy and Germany and France and all that. What do the Japanese make of it, do you think?

MUGGERIDGE: I've got a certain slight theory about it. I think that people have a certain image of a country, and they like to have that image fulfilled.

WODEHOUSE: Yes.

MUGGERIDGE: And your image is what they would like to think England was, in fact isn't, and in a sense never was. How far were you consciously satirical?

WODEHOUSE: Oh, not at all.

MUGGERIDGE: I feel you are.

WODEHOUSE: I don't like satire at all.

MUGGERIDGE: But in your picture of life there is a satirical theme.

WODEHOUSE: I suppose in a way – sort of exaggerating certain traits, but I don't know.

MUGGERIDGE: In the war one of the German agents was dropped in England, and he was wearing spats. I love the idea of German Military Intelligence having read Wodehouse, and deducing that the way to pass as a native in England is to wear spats. This man landed, and was immediately arrested.

WODEHOUSE: Did you ever wear spats?

MUGGERIDGE: I never wore spats.

WODEHOUSE: I did.

MUGGERIDGE: You actually wore them?

WODEHOUSE: Oh rather. I used to put on my frock coat and my brother's top hat and my spats and I was set for my afternoon call.

MUGGERIDGE: You were in a bank for a time. I can't think how you managed there.

WODEHOUSE: I was the worst bank clerk there's ever been, I should think. I knew nothing about it. I couldn't make out what the thing was about at all.

MUGGERIDGE: But even then you used to write?

WODEHOUSE: Oh yes, I wrote frightfully hard in those days. I used to go back to my lodgings and write in the evenings and at night.

MUGGERIDGE: When did the thought first occur to you that you were going to be a writer?

WODEHOUSE: They tell me I was writing when I was five, but it seems rather extraordinary, doesn't it?

MUGGERIDGE: What is your life like now? Tell us your day. What time do you wake up?

WODEHOUSE: They're all exactly the same. I wake up at about

eight, and then I do about three-quarters of an hour's exercise, shave and have a bath and everything, have breakfast, and then I start work which I have to knock off at twelve because I want to see a television show called 'Love of Life', which ruins my morning's work. Then lunch. Then I take the dogs for a walk. We've got a dachshund and a boxer now, and I have to take them for a walk; and then I work again until about five, I have a cocktail, dinner – very early dinner for the sake of the help, and I generally read most of the rest of the evening. It sounds awfully dull and yet it isn't.

MUGGERIDGE: How many words do you reckon to write a day?

WODEHOUSE: Oh, I'm slowing up terribly. I used to be able to do a couple of thousand every day. Now I think I'm lucky if I do six hundred.

MUGGERIDGE: Do you revise?

WODEHOUSE: I'm always revising. I'm always re-reading the stuff and spotting a place where it needs another paragraph or another scene or something.

MUGGERIDGE: It's incredible to me. You've been writing every day, for years and years, in all circumstances?

WODEHOUSE: Yes.

MUGGERIDGE: Even in your German prison camp?

WODEHOUSE: Oh, rather, I wrote awfully well there. But I never got more than about three hundred words a day done.

MUGGERIDGE: How did you actually do it?

WODEHOUSE: Well, I was able to hire a German typewriter but I couldn't compose on it. I used to write by hand, very laboriously, and in a room with about fifty people playing ping-pong and singing and so on.

MUGGERIDGE: Were the German guards interested in it?

WODEHOUSE: Oh, they were very interested. They used to stand behind me watching me do it.

MUGGERIDGE: When you look back now to that ridiculous

row in the war – about the broadcasts in Berlin – is it a painful memory?

WODEHOUSE: No, it isn't really. I wish it hadn't happened, of course, but I don't worry about it much now.

MUGGERIDGE: Do you feel any resentment about it?

WODEHOUSE: None whatever. No, I made an ass of myself and had to pay for it.

MUGGERIDGE: I mean nobody is unpleasant about it any more?

WODEHOUSE: Nobody writes to me, and nobody I meet is. I don't know what they are like in England.

MUGGERIDGE: I know on your birthday it was fantastic. Personally I think there was quite a bit of guilt feeling too.

WODEHOUSE: Oh yes.

MUGGERIDGE: What happens I think in these rows – and I was involved in a somewhat comparable one – is that very few people have actually read what the row is about.

WODEHOUSE: Exactly.

MUGGERIDGE: Do you read much contemporary writing?

WODEHOUSE: Not very much, no.

MUGGERIDGE: What books do you read with most pleasure?

WODEHOUSE: I'm afraid mystery stories nearly always. I've got an encyclopaedic knowledge of thrillers.

MUGGERIDGE: You know such a terrific lot about Shakespeare too. Do you still read Shakespeare?

WODEHOUSE: Oh I do. Now Shakespeare I do re-read regularly about once a year.

MUGGERIDGE: The whole lot?

WODEHOUSE: Yes. How bad some of it is, isn't it?

MUGGERIDGE: Are you in any way interested in religion? That's another side of human beings.

WODEHOUSE: I'm not in the least, no.

MUGGERIDGE: Have you ever been at all religious?

WODEHOUSE: No. I never passed through that phase. They always say that when you are about fifteen or sixteen you pass through a religious phase, but I never did that.

MUGGERIDGE: You wouldn't object to Christianity, for instance.

WODEHOUSE: Oh no. I've definite views on what one's supposed to do in this world. I think you're supposed to bide by your conscience, and not hurt other people and so on, but I certainly wouldn't call myself a religious man.

MUGGERIDGE: What do you think about the after life, then?

WODEHOUSE: Well I rather lean to the spiritualistic idea. I think there is an awful lot in that.

MUGGERIDGE: What, you mean that people are still around?

WODEHOUSE: Yes.

MUGGERIDGE: That they communicate?

WODEHOUSE: Yes, I think so. There seems to be so much evidence for it. But I really don't know anything about anything in that line. I'm just hopeful.

MUGGERIDGE: Would it worry you if you knew that when you died, that was the complete and total end of you?

WODEHOUSE: Oh no, not in the least.

MUGGERIDGE: Have you ever suffered from boredom at all?

WODEHOUSE: Never. Now that is rather remarkable. I can't remember a time when I was bored.

MUGGERIDGE: Were your school days happy?

WODEHOUSE: Awfully. That seems very unfashionable now, doesn't it?

MUGGERIDGE: I think it's marvellous. I think that a man like you who has work that he likes doing, that he does incomparably well, and finds the circumstances of human life delightful, and is not bored, is a very fortunate man.

WODEHOUSE: Oh, I've always been very lucky. . . .

Is an Élite Necessary?

A discussion with Lord James of Rusholme, formerly High Master of Manchester Grammar School and Vice-Chancellor of the University of York, and Bertrand Russell

MUGGERIDGE: I'm terribly sceptical about this whole business of an élite. Of course I think in any sort of society, whatever its nature, you get people who have an enormous desire for power and they will grab power – they'll find some means of getting it. If it's a money society, they'll get a lot of money, and if it's a Communist society, they'll become members of the Communist Party and get power. The thing in them is the desire for power. But I'm terribly sceptical about this idea that you can sit down and say, 'We want an élite, that is how we're going to produce it.'

JAMES: It isn't only political power. It is really in some ways the setting of values and standards for the rest of society. I disagree, I think, probably with Muggeridge over this. He has shown the whole weakness of the people who say 'We don't want an élite' by admitting that some people will grab power. I think the fundamental point about a democracy is that it must organise itself in such a way that the right people – the people who deserve it, who will exercise it rightly – have the positions of authority.

MUGGERIDGE: Well I think that's crying for the moon.

RUSSELL: I think the desire for power is by no means evidence that a man ought to have power. Quite clearly Hitler had an enormous desire for power and it didn't do any good that he should have it. What you want is some way of sifting out people according to their capacity to do a job, but I don't think that it ought to apply to the politician. I think that politics in a narrower sense ought to be still the place where the plain man's opinions count. I think it's the executive jobs where you want the élite.

JAMES: I entirely agree, because in the classical idea of the élite, I mean Plato's *Republic*, there his guardians specifically don't want power, it's one of their characteristics of course, rightly or wrongly.

MUGGERIDGE: Well I don't want to be purely obstructionist but I think that in any circumstances it would be terribly easy to define, as Plato did, the sort of people you want as your élite, and I know exactly that I would like to be governed always by humane, kindly, delightful, intelligent people, but I think that when you've said that, you've said absolutely nothing. In fact that isn't how the world works, and I myself am terribly sceptical about this idea that you sit down and say 'Now if we can produce people who have passed this exam, or people who have passed this intelligence test, or people who are born into this particular class, that is our élite.'

RUSSELL: I agree with you as against Plato's guardians because I think Plato was quite unrealistic in supposing that the guardians would not grab power. I think they would have grabbed power and presently, as one has seen in Russia, they will also grab money. I said in 1920 that Russia was exactly Plato's republic and it shocked the Platonists and shocked the Russians, but I still think it was true.

MUGGERIDGE: And enormously to your credit that you said it in my humble opinion.

RUSSELL: When I was in Russia in 1920 they complained that the only people they could get to do the work of bank clerks were ordinary seamen because everybody else was against the banks and of course the ordinary seamen didn't do the sums right.

JAMES: What is your alternative, Muggeridge, to this idea? I mean are you just going to leave those setting standards for the whole society, the possession of this executive power, that Russell was talking about, are you going to leave that just to the naked operation of the market?

MUGGERIDGE: In a sense yes. I myself take the view that power is an abhorrent thing, and it's a most unfortunate circumstance of life that it's necessary to have people to exert power. I'd much prefer to live in a world in which that wasn't so, but since I have to recognise that it is so, I am inclined to think that what you've got to do is to let those people who want it and want it desperately get it, and I think that all your arrangements, which of course nowadays are very popular, for training people and picking them out and having intelligence tests and character tests, ultimately will prove a complete failure.

JAMES: But I'm sure that your whole idea of power is much too narrow a one. You're thinking of it entirely in terms of political power.

MUGGERIDGE: I'm not.

JAMES: In the modern set-up what you've got to think of is the administrator – professional administrator – who's not obviously a sort of man who loves power or enjoys the exercise of it. You've got further the scientist and the technologist. You've got further the person who in the aesthetic and general culture field sets the standard for a great ignorant democracy. Now those people are exercising great power.

MUGGERIDGE: I quite agree.

JAMES: But they don't call it power.

MUGGERIDGE: I don't think you can choose them.

RUSSELL: Take a perfectly concrete thing. Take agriculture. The amount of agricultural land in England is small in proportion to the population and it's very desirable that the agricultural land should be profitably farmed. Now, the immense majority of farmers have an absolute contempt for scientific agriculture and unless you compel or induce them they will ignore everything that is known about how land should be farmed and that ought not to be allowed.

MUGGERIDGE: Try as you will to arrive at those people who can most usefully cultivate the very limited land in this country, in fact the people who will most usefully cultivate it will be the people who want to cultivate it primarily for reasons, alas, of cupidity.

JAMES: Well I'm sorry but that isn't really true today any longer. You see, if you take Russell's example, which is a very good one, of agriculture, there is a new class of technologists who are not going to make anything more than a salary out of it. They represent the new élite as it were.

MUGGERIDGE: Well, I believe in the naked operation of human passion.

JAMES: You have a democratic educational system in which you attempt as far as possible to give some sort of opportunity to every person whatever their background; and you choose those people who are more intelligent than other people, and you give them a different sort of education.

MUGGERIDGE: Well I would only say this, that if the affairs of our country were flourishing at this moment, our foreign service was distinguishing itself in every part of the world, then I think James's proposition would stand up very well, but what I discover as a journalist wandering about this world is that these people in fact know absolutely nothing about what they're supposed to be doing. They were all chosen, they've all got through this mesh, they've all distinguished themselves in this terrific process for choosing an élite. My goodness how badly they're doing – how badly they're doing.

JAMES: Good gracious, what an extraordinary picture of the world you have if I may say so. How long do you think we've had real secondary education in this country. Fifty-four years, and you see it hasn't grown up in that time.

MUGGERIDGE: The thing is that this system of choosing an élite by means of intellectual tests has operated now for quite a time and in my opinion it has been a total failure.

RUSSELL: It seems to me that our Civil Service is imperfect because we still attach too much importance to a classical education and not enough to science.

MUGGERIDGE: Yes, but the methods that we're adopting, and I'm sure they're most honourably conceived, are in fact methods which do not catch the right people.

JAMES: Oh I see. It's the methods now, not the principle.

MUGGERIDGE: Yes, of course it's the methods. You set up certain examinations, certain tests, and you say, I will apply those tests and I will produce splendid, brilliant, effective administrators; and I say to you that those particular people that you choose have in actual practice not done very well, and it occurs to me that because they haven't done very well, this whole idea of choosing people in that way may not be the right system.

JAMES: I want to know what's wrong with the methods.

MUGGERIDGE: What's wrong with the methods is that you are basing your tests primarily on intelligence.

RUSSELL: All men have equal rights in certain respects, but that doesn't mean that they are equal. I mean, nobody would maintain that everybody is fit to be Prime Minister.

MUGGERIDGE: I would use the simple method that the man who wishes to exert power gets power.

JAMES: But that gives us Hitler.

MUGGERIDGE: Yes. It gives us Napoleon, it gives us Lenin, it gives us Roosevelt, it gives us all the people who've exercised power in our time. But I hate them all because I hate power.

JAMES: You must admit that they're all pretty intelligent.

MUGGERIDGE: Yes, but they'd have failed in the Manchester Grammar School.

JAMES: Have you any conceivable evidence for that whatever? Have you any idea what the Manchester Grammar School exam is like?

RUSSELL: We know that Napoleon was quite a good mathematician.

MUGGERIDGE: Where I think that this whole business of an élite goes wrong is that it's a dream. It's the same dream as the platonic dream.

RUSSELL: It isn't a dream. If you take the ordinary person whose IQ is, we'll say, 90 and compare him with a person whose IQ is 120, nobody can deny that there is a difference which is quite obvious; and if you put the man whose IQ is 90 in a position of power, he will infallibly make a mess of it. The first man may, but he certainly will.

MUGGERIDGE: But is it really true, Lord Russell, that the man with the high IQ is good at his job? The only man of action I've ever cared for is Lincoln who was a very attractive person; and I always remember that wonderful story about him and Grant, who was a drunkard. People said, 'This is a terrible thing, you've got a General who's a drunkard', and Lincoln said, 'Grant wins battles and I wish all my Generals were drunkards'. This seems to me the essence of the thing, that if you've got Generals you want them to win battles, and you don't care whether they're frightfully good at the Staff College.

JAMES: What has that got to do with it? What we're saying is that on the whole Generals will win battles when they're more intelligent. I mean the number of battles that have been lost by a jolly good, pure ivory-headed chap must be absolutely legion. Your argument really rests on misconception about this idea of intelligence. Would you be interested to know that in the last war 95 per cent of the subalterns were drawn from the top five per cent of the population as regards intelligence. But you wouldn't really think that subalterns were intellectuals would you?

MUGGERIDGE: Speaking of my own small experience of the war, I really can't mention names here, but of two Generals one was a complete failure and was intellectually very distinguished, and the other was fantastically successful and was, from a purely intellectual point of view, one of the most foolish men I've ever met.

JAMES: By your standards.

MUGGERIDGE: By any standards.

JAMES: He was probably in the top five per cent of the population.

MUGGERIDGE: Oh not at all.

JAMES: He would certainly have been to the staff college.

MUGGERIDGE: Minor point, minor point. But the fact is, you see, I think these particular tests that you apply do not measure people who are capable of doing this mysterious and abhorrent thing of governing and controlling their fellows.

JAMES: What I am saying is that high intelligence is not a sufficient criterion; it is a necessary prerequisite.

Even More Education
Education gives me an odd nightmare from time to time. I occasionally dream I'm on an Any Questions? *programme in a studio deep underground, and up on the surface the last vestiges of western civilisation are coming to an end, the mushroom cloud is forming. We are discussing the increase in juvenile delinquency, and a peeress in her own right gets up and says, 'What we need is more and better education'. At that minute I always wake up screaming.*

Equality
On the one hand we are telling people that it is absolutely wrong that there should be any inequality, and any honest man must assent to that. On the other hand, we are asking people to save, to provide for their future, to pursue their own interests and ends. Now these two things are, in fact, incompatible.

Television

Just imagine! At this very moment all over the world – by the muddy banks of tropical rivers, in remote deserts and tangled jungle and frozen Arctic wastes – people are watching *Peyton Place*. Or, if that hasn't reached them yet, some old print of *I Love Lucy* or *Wagon Train*. Isn't it terrific! Various attempts have been made to unify mankind – the Holy Roman Empire, the Comintern, the United Nations. Where they all failed *Batman* has succeeded; he, not the *Internationale* (as we sang in the old revolutionary hymn), unites the human race.

This universality of the telly has been all too little noticed in the celebrations of its various anniversaries. A Pope may claim to say mass for scores or even hundreds of millions of Catholics, Communist leaders in their more ebullient moments when they gather on Lenin's tomb are liable to speak of the toiling masses everywhere who look to them for guidance, but how can they compete with *The Man from UNCLE*, welcome at every hearth and home on earth, and, I daresay, in due course in the universe beyond. I feel sure that the first American astronauts to land on the moon will pipe in *UNCLE* long before they get round to Jesus Christ, or even L.B.J.

There's another thing; through this universal telly the so-called backward or under-developed nations of the world can see in advance the glorious possibilities which lie before them when they become advanced and civilised. It should prove a tremendous incentive to effort and endurance – all those wonderful pills and potions they're going to be able to swallow to cure all the wonderful ailments which are going to afflict them; all the wonderful wars and liberations, all the wonderful marriages and divorces and race-riots which lie before them. Why, they must be saying to themselves, if we work hard at our studies and pay due attention to what the

Peace Corps man tells us, we'll be able to read *Peyton Place* as well as see it on the telly. If that thought doesn't get them moving along the road to progress and prosperity, then nothing will.

This is the first time in human history that, thanks to television, the uncivilised have been presented with a visual preview of what civilisation holds in store for them. One likes to think that, had the Goths and Vandals been able to envisage Governor Reagan, H. Wilson, the Beatles and other choice twentieth-century items, they would have tiptoed back to their forest fastnesses and stayed there instead of advancing on Rome. I fear, however, that no such caution will operate today. *Lone Ranger*, *Lucy*, *Batman* and *The Man from UNCLE* may be expected, alas, only to urge backward viewers on to the blessedness which beckons, with the Gross National Product for ever rising, the electorate for ever voting, muzak for ever sounding and neon for ever shining.

TV Addiction
The only thing to do is to follow me and have your aerials removed; a very simple operation, it doesn't hurt in any way, and you'll feel infinitely better for it.

174

The Problem of Pain

A discussion with Archbishop Anthony Bloom
of the Russian Orthodox Church

MUGGERIDGE: I suppose it would be true to say that in the modern world the tendency is to try and pretend that pain doesn't exist at all. I read once about a French king who thought that, if he was never confronted with the sight of a funeral, there would be no death, and I feel that somehow, by means of drugs and an attitude of mind, people try to pretend there's no such thing as pain. Do you agree with that?

BLOOM: Yes, I think there are two tendencies in the modern world which are equally wrong. The one is to pretend that things which do exist do not exist, because they are too painful to face; and the other one is, when they come your way because you cannot avoid it, simply to do away with them artificially. Pain-killers, tranquillisers, anything provided you do not face up to what is real.

MUGGERIDGE: Then, Archbishop, why is there pain in the universe? I think this is one of the greatest stumbling blocks today to people believing in religion at all. Why should there be this thing – pain?

BLOOM: Well, I think that you cannot answer that kind of question from the point of view of the believer while remaining on the ground of the unbeliever. One can argue about a system from within, and what those of us who believe in a personal God do believe is that the world, as we see it now, is not the world as God made and willed it. It is the free will of men that has introduced into it qualities, characteristics which do not belong to it originally. You may, of course, say – Why did God create man free? It would be so nice if nothing wrong had happened simply because nothing could happen. But then there would have been nothing good, either, because love, for instance, is conditioned by freedom. You may say that God has taken a risk, if you reason from man's point of view – the point of view of one who doesn't know the final outcome. But I would say God knew what He was doing, knew that it was worth the cost, and if you turn to certain saints they will answer the same – a man like St Seraphim of Sarov, who is a Russian saint who died in the middle of the nineteenth century, said that since he knew God he could say it was worth suffering, for thousands of years, every moment of one's life, in order to know Him.

MUGGERIDGE: To know that moment of ecstasy. Of course. Although not a particular believer myself, I feel that this is so. I think this horror of pain is a rather low instinct and that if I think of human beings I've known and of my own life, such as it is, I can't recall any case of pain which didn't, on the whole, enrich life.

BLOOM: I think it always does enrich life, and people who try to escape it from cowardice miss something extremely precious.

MUGGERIDGE: I think we ought also to take a concrete case. For instance, a person shrieking, howling in agony – the last stages of cancer, or something like that, or maybe an imbecile, a drooling imbecile. Along comes a materialist and says that such a life is now worth nothing, it should be painlessly ended. What about that?

BLOOM: Well, there is an old Russian saying that one should never take away what one cannot give back, and I think no human being is allowed to take life, because he cannot give it back, and he cannot even condition life.

MUGGERIDGE: So even as a doctor, which you were, you would say that it is never permissible to put out a life?

BLOOM: No, I think it is never permissible to put out a life.

MUGGERIDGE: And that the mere putting out of a life is a sin in all circumstances?

BLOOM: Yes, I think it's a wrong done to the person, which does not mean that you must not apply all your knowledge, all your skill, all your sympathy to make life more bearable and suffering less excruciating.

MUGGERIDGE: Of course, I wholly agree. I think that regarding human beings who are incapacitated as not entitled to live – which the Nazis embodied in legislation – is utterly horrible. But then let's take a borderline case. Let's imagine someone who is in great physical agony, and to ease that agony you must administer drugs. But by so doing you know as a doctor that you may very well be ending the patient's life. It could be so, I imagine.

BLOOM: Yes, it could.

MUGGERIDGE: How would you decide that dilemma?

BLOOM: I think you cannot impose on a man more than he can bear, and you can, you must bring him to the very edge of what is bearable. Yet you must do all you can to avoid his losing consciousness unnecessarily, which I think is done very often because people think that if a patient is unconscious he suffers less and his death will come in an easier way. This I think is wrong. But there is another thing which strikes me. In all these discussions (and this is implicit in your own question) there is an assumption that the person will not face up to pain. There is an assumption that every person is a coward, every person is incapable of rising to the level of great human courage. And I think this is unjust. I have met more than once people who seem to be the most ordinary kind of men and women, and who when confronted with tragedy were simply heroic.

And in particular, the case of a woman whom I had known very young, who happened to have a cancer of the breast, which was an acute cancer and developed within a very short time. She was a very simple believer, and she said, 'If God has sent me the suffering, there must be meaning in it, and there must also be strength in store for me.' And she refused to be helped by drugs. Up to the point when her chest was completely destroyed and one could see her lung breathing through the wound, until one day she woke and said, 'This night the Lord Christ has come close to me, and now it does not matter whether I suffer, or whether you help me out of it, because I have learned all I need to learn from it.' And she accepted alleviation. She acted exactly to the contrary of what people usually do, or assume they would do.

MUGGERIDGE: That is very interesting. Of course, the Western church did oppose the use of anaesthetics, didn't it. Did the Eastern church do that too?

BLOOM: No, but I don't think it was for virtue's sake. It was simply ignorance, and partly, it didn't come into the scope of its activity.

MUGGERIDGE: Do you think there was any sense at all in that opposition to the use of anaesthetics?

BLOOM: No, I don't think so. I think that a man should be offered every possibility there is to suffer less, but should also be taught and given courage to face up to much more than we usually do.

MUGGERIDGE: But you must have seen a large number of people die?

BLOOM: Yes, I have in fact.

MUGGERIDGE: We've lived through a lot of death in our time one way and another. And I imagine that people die very differently, I mean their mood when they die. Do you think that lots of people bitterly fear and dread death? Do you find that in your experience?

BLOOM: I think that Westerners seem to dread death much more than, say, the Russians. One of the things that impresses me in the Western attitude to death is that it is considered almost indecent to die. One should do that on the quiet. And when someone has died one hides him away, the children are not allowed to come and say a last goodbye to their parents or grandparents, and I find it shocking. What I find so often is that people should have been taught about death when they were full of sap and life, and when they could still face death not as a terror but as a challenge.

MUGGERIDGE: Of course, you see, Archbishop, death is the stranger at the feast of materialism and affluence. In America you know they make up corpses, they put lipstick on them, it is carried to the very limit; this pretence that it doesn't happen.

BLOOM: Yes exactly.

MUGGERIDGE: But I was thinking also of confronting the pain that goes with death. Do you find human beings predominantly cowardly or predominantly courageous?

BLOOM: I remember an admirable answer which was reported in the life of the French curé d'Ars concerning a sick child he was visiting; he said: 'Child, how can you bear your pain?' and the child smiled and said, 'Father, I have learnt to bear only the pain of the present moment. I don't feel any more yesterday's pain, nor yet tomorrow's.'

MUGGERIDGE: I think it applies also to happiness.

BLOOM: To everything.

MUGGERIDGE: I mean that the man who is thinking of tomorrow's happiness or yesterday's happiness is perhaps missing the whole idea of happiness.

BLOOM: Well, we miss everything when we cannot live in the present moment where the thing is real.

MUGGERIDGE: Yes, I'm sure that's right. I'm sure that's right. When people say how can there be a loving God, if the human race should be subjected to such tortures and miseries and destruction in so short a space of time, as we've seen, what do you say to people who say that?

BLOOM: Well there is a passage in the writing of the French theologian, John Danielou, that impressed me very greatly recently. He says something like: 'Suffering is the only meeting point between good and evil and the only chance for the evil one to be saved by the innocent.' And if you give more thought to it, you come to the conclusion that if good and evil never met, that is, if there was never suffering inflicted on the innocent by evil in general, or by an evil person in particular, there would be two parallel lines, the one of utter

179

damnation, and the other one of salvation. But the law of life as we see it in nature, in human relationships, is that whenever one is evil someone who is innocent will suffer. One has drunk before he drove his car, and this child has been killed. I have been irresponsible before I performed an operation, and I have overlooked something of importance, and so on. This meeting point between the sufferer and the one who inflicts suffering is a point of crucial importance. It is the crossroads, it's also a cross, a real crucifixion at times. And the moment you suffer either great suffering or trivial suffering at the hand of someone and can forgive, you manifest really divine power.

MUGGERIDGE: You could apply that then to collective events. You could say the Nazis burnt up and killed six million Jews, the Stalinists killed three million peasants, and so on, and the fact of this, our wickedness resulting in this suffering, can purge the wickedness? Have I got that right?

BLOOM: Yes, I think I can give you an example, taken from a concentration camp, a prayer left on a sheet of wrapping paper, which in substance says: 'O Lord remember not only the men of goodwill but also the men of ill will. But do not remember all the suffering they have inflicted on us, remember the fruits we have gathered, thanks to this suffering – our comradeship, our loyalty, our humility, the courage, the generosity, the greatness of heart which has grown out of this, and when they come to judgement, let all the fruits which we have borne be their forgiveness.'

MUGGERIDGE: Therefore suffering is not a horrible thing necessarily? But a necessary thing, and sometimes an ennobling and elevating thing – is that right?

BLOOM: I think it is ennobling and I think it is creative, but it may be nonsense if you do not see meaning or put meaning into it. The mere fact of suffering does not make you a martyr.

Some little while ago I had a very edifying conversation on the telly about the problem of pain with a very distinguished and holy Orthodox Bishop, who like all orthodox bishops had a big black beard. And I thought we'd gone rather deeply into this subject. Imagine my surprise when the following day I got a taxi and the taxi driver said to me: 'I saw you yesterday with that bloke with a beard – you knocked hell out of him.' So don't worry, nobody's listening.

Slippery Path
Seeing the fall of Man as a celestial banana skin joke makes everything comprehensible.

Advertising
If you are going to advertise it's almost certain that you'll exaggerate, and therefore ninety per cent of advertising is lies.

In America particularly, some of the best brains, the best endeavour in the country is being devoted solely to persuading people to want what they don't want, to get rid of things before they're worn out, to buy other things that are totally unnecessary, and it's only by all that activity that this mad society can run.

Ladies and Gentlemen, it is my pleasure

Reflections on an American Lecture Tour

The day has come round again. From every corner of the globe, we, the L men, are converging on New York. The American lecture season is about to open. Ladies in Eau Claire Wisconsin await my coming. Santa Maria California, do not lose heart – I'll be with you soon. Jewish ladies in Los Angeles – Executives in Seattle – Art lovers in Chicago – I'm on my way.

The American appetite to be addressed is inexhaustible. From us a message; from them a dollar. Hungry sheep look up and are, one hopes, duly fed. A lecture tour is perpetual motion. In trains, in aeroplanes, in motor-cars, one's ancient carcase is relentlessly transported to and fro, and up and down, America. At Gettysburg this weird odyssey begins. Ah – if only it was possible to be as brief as Lincoln!

America is largely made of cardboard, which at night shines and blinks with deceptive neon, wonderful to behold. If only, as G. K. Chesterton remarked, one couldn't read. Endlessly repeated exhortations to eat, to drink, to sleep, perchance to dream. Banners of a vast consumer's army bravely held aloft. 'Onward affluent soldiers, marching as to war, with the "national product" going on before.' Such is the approach to every American city. Ahead, emerging like mountain peaks, the central core of skyscrapers.

The thing Americans most like doing, I always think, is driving a big car along one of their highways – mile after mile, hour after hour. No means of knowing where you are; not in a sense going through the country at all – going through nothingness, as though the motion itself produces a sense of restfulness.

Not long ago I was driving across this country from coast to coast, and arrived at a small town, a tiny American town, late at night. And I saw four neon signs standing out in the darkness. One of these signs said 'gas', one said 'beauty', one said 'food', and one said 'drugs', and with a feeling of absolute exultation I realised that these were the four pillars of the modern world. This was the American way of life. A super-abundance of gas, and food, and beauty and drugs.

Americans often seem like a looting army. They, as it were, invade and occupy their own country, gorging their own provisions, sacking their own cities, grabbing their own treasure, raping their own women. Will they perhaps in the end repulse the invading hordes – themselves – winning a glorious victory in self-destruction?

If I were a woman, I'd rather be a whore than a bunny.

The American Way of Sex

Sex is the mysticism of materialism and the only possible religion in a materialistic society. In America today the religion of sex has reached its highest point of development and attracted the largest number of adherents. The devout dedicate their lives to sex, from the cradle to the grave and even beyond. The sacred pornographic texts, from *Kama Sutra* to *Fanny Hill*, *Chatterley*, the *Cancers* and *Candy*, edify the faithful. As do film goddesses, seen through a camera lens brightly, black or white or in glorious technicolor. Eat this, wear this, anoint yourself with this, in remembrance of sex. Even the cadavers are perfumed and pomaded in case there should be a chance for a tumble in the coffin and dating through eternity. Rarely if ever in history has a religion attracted adherents so zealous and so numerous. It is of sex that cherubim and seraphim continually do sing. In the beginning was the Flesh, and the Flesh became Word. In the spoken and the written word, in neon signs, on rotary presses, on the waves of sound and light that overflow the ether, the new evangel is joyously proclaimed – to die in the spirit and be reborn in the flesh.

Sex sells anything from deodorants to bulldozers. It's the magic ingredient, the packaged thrill, the plastic glow. Oh, vestal virgins of Madison Avenue. Oh, Aphrodite, rising so fragrantly, so exquisitely out of the mist of universal desire. Even the dolls must have reached puberty to be interesting. The bra precedes the breast.

To the outward eye, a campus in Ohio presents an idyllic scene. There are young co-eds bound as to the tabor's sound. Where in the wide world would you find such artlessness combined with such earnestness? The sorority houses are aviaries where the singing birds try out their fledgling wings. Freed now from parental control, still liable to be strict in these Middle-Western regions, these are the nurseries, the learner slopes in the great pursuit of happiness on which Americans, and following them mankind, are bent. Blithely and innocently prepared for the long littleness of sex, with youth at the steering-wheel, and pleasure in the rear seat, they're all agog. On their heads, just and unjust, the erotic persuasion of advertisers, pundits and pornographers falls like black atomic rain.

Each separate elegant home, each lush convertible is a temple dedicated to the cult of sex, to the assiduous practice of *erotica domestica*. Sex is pleasure, marriage is virtue, and ever the twain shall meet. Marriage is a Grecian urn whose lovers, though they may not be outwardly for ever young, must engage in transports that are for ever fresh. Many willing hands and minds assist them. Nor need the coming of the menopause, the passage of years, the decay of the body, the dropping out of hair and teeth, abate their ardour. Let me not to the marriage of true bodies admit impediment. In sickness and in health, till death them do part, they may continue to pursue happiness in one another's arms. Oh, sex, where is thy sting?

Human Activity
The two most ridiculous activities in which I've ever been engaged have been war and sex.

Entente Concordiale
I was delighted to hear that Concorde was going to land at Dallas airport, Washington – a unique spectacle of one white elephant on another white elephant, which as far as I know has never happened in the world before.

The Road to Canterbury

An Ursuline Nun's vocation

MUGGERIDGE: Of course from the point of view of the normal twentieth-century standards you've given up everything that people think makes life worthwhile.

SISTER MARY THOMAS: Yes, but you see, if I may say so I think this is typical of your attitude, Malcolm. You always look at the negative side of things. You don't see what I've gained. Take for instance the vow of chastity which of course intrigues everybody, this terrible thing that I've done, that I've given up –

MUGGERIDGE: I don't think that, incidentally –

SISTER MARY THOMAS: No – all right – but for me the vow of chastity has such a positive aspect as well as the negative; it's not just a question of what I've given up. You see, I have these natural instincts, womanly maternal instincts, which are thoroughly good in themselves, and which simply mustn't be stunted. I mustn't give them up. I must on the contrary develop them to the full, I must be a woman to the full, but I don't do this by developing them towards one person and one small family. If you like to put it in this way, I have this spiritual procreation with Christ through my union with Christ whose spouse I am. I bring forth children to Christ through union with Him in the spiritual way, and this is something more, much wider, much less exclusive and much more creative.

MUGGERIDGE: I think I can understand that. I mean personally of course. You're always hauling me over the coals for saying so, but I think that the things you've given up for the most part are not worth having.

SISTER MARY THOMAS: Yes, but you see Malcolm, you've got

186

to keep both feet on the ground all the same. You're living in this world.

MUGGERIDGE: Well that's an inescapable fact.

SISTER MARY THOMAS: Yes, but it seems to me that you're always trying to get too much out of this world.

MUGGERIDGE: I'm trying to look beyond it. Is that a wicked thing to do?

SISTER MARY THOMAS: Well, I think you go too far; you see you don't seem to want the world at all. It seems to me you're like a shipwrecked man who finds himself in the water, and when he finds an opposition between the water and his body, he panics and fights and tries to get out of the water, to climb out of the water into the air. Well of course he can't do this, and so he drowns. But if he just changes his attitude he finds that this opposition will remain between the water and his body, but he can make it creative and he can float and make something creative out of the opposition, and he's saved.

Death on the Roads

The truth is that one of the most squalid and horrible things about the manner in which we live is our acceptance of this toll of life on the roads. I'm perfectly certain that future historians looking back will think that it was one of the most dreadful and callous things that's ever been, and I'm equally certain that it will not be stopped, or even prevented from increasing, until far more drastic action is taken. But if our cant about being a free society and regarding human life as the most precious thing meant anything at all we should do those drastic things.

Christianity and Politics

A conversation with Trevor Huddleston,
now Bishop of Mauritius

MUGGERIDGE: 'Should a Christian keep out of politics?' is one of those very profound and important questions about which one doesn't naturally feel inclined to be dogmatic. Now we're going to take the particular case, at any rate to begin with, of Father Huddleston who is not only a Christian but a Christian priest. He wears the uniform of his church and, to some extent at any rate, his church is committed by what he does. And he felt bound – as probably most viewers know – in South Africa to take a certain very definite line politically, about apartheid. Now we're not discussing the goodness or badness of that. What we're discussing is whether someone like Father Huddleston, a Christian, a priest, is wise to identify himself with certain political movements and certain political activities whose end of course can't be foreseen, which might end in ways which would be very repugnant to him, but at the moment seem to him to represent goodness as against badness.

Now, Father Huddleston, I'm going to begin by the simplest possible question. Do you feel yourself that the action you took was right or wrong?

HUDDLESTON: I think I can honestly say I believe the action I took was right. I believe that I was caught in a particular situation in which human rights were involved, and of course it's very difficult to distinguish exactly between human rights and political rights.

MUGGERIDGE: Could you give us an example of action as distinct from a point of view?

HUDDLESTON: Yes, I think so. I was involved in trying to prevent the Government implementing the Western Areas

188

Removal Scheme – a scheme which involved the uprooting of some seventy thousand Africans from their homes, expropriating their property, and placing them in a different locality. Now the Government maintained that this was a slum clearance scheme. I maintained that it was part of the apartheid policy, in other words that the removal was not done from motives of bettering the African people but simply because it was in pursuance of a racial policy, and I felt and still feel that racialism is something wholly incompatible with the Christian faith. Therefore I felt bound by any means in my power, short of immoral ones, to oppose it.

MUGGERIDGE: But you did feel it right to identify yourself with action, with political action, taken in protest against that.

HUDDLESTON: Yes I most certainly did and looking back I still would feel that I could have done nothing else, and if I were in the same position tomorrow I would do the same thing.

MUGGERIDGE: I would like to ask you about a thing that's often puzzled me in relation to this whole problem. In the time, for instance, of St Paul there was the problem of slavery –

HUDDLESTON: Yes – certainly.

MUGGERIDGE: – and we all know that slavery is a vile thing, and various attempts were made to persuade St Paul to declare himself on that issue, which attempts, as I understand, he resisted. In other words, what he did was to preach a gospel which of course in the end made slavery inconceivable, but he didn't identify himself with a movement – an immediate and local movement against slavery. Now wasn't he perhaps right in that?

HUDDLESTON: Well I think, of course, he was right, but there was no movement with which he could identify himself. But where St Paul speaks very clearly about slavery, as a matter of fact, is in the Epistle to Philemon, which is an epistle written to a slave owner about a Christian slave, and the whole foundation of that letter is, I think, one of the most moving and telling arguments against slavery in the whole Christian armour.

MUGGERIDGE: Without identifying himself with an anti-slavery movement?

HUDDLESTON: Yes, simply because there was no question of such a movement existing, but when the anti-slavery movement did come into existence in the time of Wilberforce in this country, Christians had to choose.

MUGGERIDGE: Well, that's my whole point – what St Paul had preached, as it were, came to fruition?

HUDDLESTON: Yes, but there were plenty of Christians who denied that there was any need whatsoever to argue for the abolition of slavery. In fact, if you read the debates in the House on that particular subject –

MUGGERIDGE: There were Christians who failed –

HUDDLESTON: It was very much the Bishops, I'm afraid, who did argue very strongly that slavery was perfectly reasonable.

MUGGERIDGE: Now could I put another one. The Jews were subject people and the Romans were colonialists. Wasn't a tremendous pressure put on our Lord to identify Himself with that nationalist movement and didn't He resist it?

HUDDLESTON: Yes, you're perfectly correct I'm sure there. I mean, you've only to think of Palm Sunday and the opportunity it would have given to our Lord to proclaim Himself the kind of King that the nationalists wanted. Nevertheless, you've got to remember that the Crucifixion was a political act, and our Lord, when He was questioned, as He was by Pilate, and when He was faced with this question – 'Art Thou a King then?' – didn't make any attempt whatsoever to explain His position away. If He had done Pilate could, and would no doubt, have released Him.

MUGGERIDGE: This terrific thing is not a new thing or a new dilemma for man, and in fact it arose in a very dramatic and immediate way during our Lord's life when He was asked, presumably by some cunning person who wanted to trip Him up, 'Should we give tribute to Caesar' – and He made the marvellous answer 'Render unto Caesar the things that are Caesar's and unto God the things that are God's'. Like all wonderful answers it doesn't really answer. Father Huddleston, would you agree that is the absolute nub of the thing?

HUDDLESTON: I would say this, that our Lord deliberately gave an equivocal answer because as He looked forward through the centuries He saw that at certain times in history it would be most necessary to render unto God the things that are God's, and therefore the emphasis there is more on how we are to be quite certain that we are rendering to God the things that are God's. Surely what is absolutely vital in society is that man, created in the image and likeness of God, should be able to find and fulfil himself as a person. In other words, that the state is made for man and not man for the state, and therefore, if the church is to be true to her vocation she's got to go on insisting that certain things belong to God and nobody else.

Appointment With:

A conversation with Stephen Spender, Cyril Connolly,
Wystan H. Auden and Christopher Isherwood in March 1962

MUGGERIDGE: By happy chance, these four writers who dominated the thirties find themselves in London together after many travels, vicissitudes and adventures; and, of course, the first thought one has about them is the change from that time. Stephen, you've been connected with Cyril's magazine *Horizon*, a literary magazine, a very difficult thing to run in this country. And now you're running another one – *Encounter.* Is it very different?

SPENDER: Yes, I think one of the paradoxical things is that the 1930s was a much more literary period; it was more possible to have a purely literary magazine because there was this exciting experimental writing going on. Today I think that, although there's less concern with politics, nevertheless a magazine has to have more discussion of general affairs in it, which is what has really made *Encounter* rather successful.

MUGGERIDGE: You mean you have to have more about politics although people are less interested in it?

SPENDER: Yes, or perhaps it's simply that literature seems less exciting, less experimental now, and there's more interest in the social context in which we're living rather than the political context.

MUGGERIDGE: I feel Cyril is in a different category really because he is very much the same person – the only incorruptible.

CONNOLLY: I was corrupt before anybody else had started.

MUGGERIDGE: How do you account for that, Cyril, that these fellow writers of yours have all undergone such tremendous changes and you really remain ploughing the same furrow?

CONNOLLY: Well, I think because I'm just a little bit older. I grew up more in the twenties than in the thirties; in other words, the twenties gave me a bias towards independence. Unimpressed by political slogans to some extent, love of pleasure, perhaps, which is now called frivolity and is much attacked; but on the whole I already had a personality before I fell under the influence of these three people who have had a devastating influence on me.

MUGGERIDGE: Have you shaken it off now?

CONNOLLY: I wish I had, but I haven't. It still remains.

MUGGERIDGE: In what way?

CONNOLLY: Well, chiefly that I'm rather ashamed of myself for not being sterner all the time. When I first knew them, you see – I met Wystan in Spain through Christopher and they were political mentors – I wanted to be an extremely

Left-Wing, Socialist-minded writer, and I carried this balloon of 1920s frivolity behind me, which I was trying to pop all the time; I hoped they'd pop it for me.

MUGGERIDGE: Did they?

CONNOLLY: Almost, yes. But then they began to backslide. If Wystan had remained the author of the poem on Spain, if Christopher had remained the strong Left-Wing sort of commissar he was, and if even Stephen had remained what he set out to be when he wrote *Forward from Liberalism*, I think I would be a fierce, middle-aged Labour Member of Parliament now.

SPENDER: Well, I think it was mutual; you've helped a good deal to free us from our ideologies.

MUGGERIDGE: But Stephen, take, for instance, this book *Forward from Liberalism* – the idea there, as I recall, was that the logical thing for a Liberal to become was a Communist?

SPENDER: Yes.

MUGGERIDGE: But you've relinquished this idea?

SPENDER: Yes I have, because I think the reason why I wanted that was simply that the Communists were playing the most effective role against Fascism; all the other people were really quite ineffective, weren't they, or seemed to be. I, therefore, allowed myself to overlook certain things about Communism, like the trials in Russia of the people who were supposed to be the enemies of Stalin.

AUDEN: But Stephen, I think we were frightfully snobbish there, you know, because we quite simply thought that Russians weren't white folk and couldn't be expected to behave properly. We didn't like it very much but we thought, well it'll be quite different in the West. I blame myself rather much for that.

MUGGERIDGE: Wystan, do you feel now that your political views then were wrong?

AUDEN: No. Not with regard to what one thought was happening in Europe. No.

SPENDER: No, I think what one rather regrets is not having done more about them because one still thinks that given a little extra push the war might have been stopped. What could we have done more?

CONNOLLY: I don't see what could have been done except writing warning articles and so on. We couldn't *do* anything.

AUDEN: We made the mistake of thinking that writing was important. But if you say that, the only thing you can do is straight factual reporting, and then you have to know the facts, which we didn't. What's the good of writing a poem saying how awful Hitler is? It doesn't make any difference.

MUGGERIDGE: Do you really feel, Wystan – this interests me very much – that writing, as a political instrument, is not important, not effective?

AUDEN: Prose may be; I know that poetry is no use at all.

SPENDER: I don't absolutely agree. I think that, for instance, your poem 'Refugee Blues' –

AUDEN: What difference did that make?

SPENDER: Perhaps nothing made any difference –

CONNOLLY: It made refugees feel that somebody understood and cared for them. But they were already refugees, of course.

MUGGERIDGE: Christopher, my impression is that you were slightly less politically inclined than these others?

ISHERWOOD: In the thirties I was a very individualistic person who felt very strongly on certain issues but was, fundamentally, not a joiner.

SPENDER: None of us were joiners, then or now.

MUGGERIDGE: And yet you *did* join.

ISHERWOOD: As a matter of fact I didn't actually join anything at all; we were only, as it were, adding to the chorus.

MUGGERIDGE: What about the new writers we get when we turn in the old ones?

SPENDER: I think the young writers of today are the fulfilment of a prophesy in the thirties, that there ought to be some kind of working-class literature which in the thirties was being written by middle-class people. In a way, Wesker, Pinter, Osborne and so on are the kind of writers in the theatre whom we were trying to be, because they know about the kind of life which we were trying to write about, and this gives them considerable authority and makes the theatre seem more genuinely experimental than poetry or the novel.

MUGGERIDGE: When I was thinking about you four last night it occurred to me that what was common to you all was this implied sense of doom, of a catastrophe that was coming, something awful – Cyril's famous remark about 'the pleasure gardens of the West', and I remember reading, Stephen, in your autobiography that from a child you always felt there was a ghastly catastrophe looming. Now do you feel this has happened?

SPENDER: I think that the catastrophe is still with us and this is simply the end of our civilisation. In the thirties, we thought that this would take the form of the triumph of Fascism; today it's the hydrogen bomb.

MUGGERIDGE: So actually the judgement day hasn't come, has it?

SPENDER: It's always there.

MUGGERIDGE: In the poems you wrote in the thirties, Wystan, one constantly returns to some terrible thing that would obliterate you – you still feel that?

AUDEN: That continues actually. I don't think I'm personally paranoiac, but I find in what I write, from the earliest period till now, a strong paranoiac imagination. Now why this is so I don't know.

SPENDER: It's a sense of final catastrophe that's peculiar to us.

AUDEN: You just have to go on and shut your eyes and say, 'Well, whatever happens, I have to write as if there would be people to read this in a hundred years' time'.

Current Reflections

The conflict Stephen Spender speaks about in that conversation between art and, say, journalism is, I think, frankly boloney. In a way the moment people are self-consciously artists there's no art. An artist is no more responsible than a dustman; he's just a man who happens to be an artist. I personally believe that when a society is breaking up the only artistic response to it is what could be called, in very general terms, 'reportage'.

And there's something else very peculiar about that conversation with these four people that I've never mentioned publicly before. There was one matter I felt I must raise with them, and I never raised it. Auden and Isherwood particularly had been extremely insistent that the time had come – echoing Mosley – for action, the requisite action being to fight the fascists. But the moment England and France lurched into war against Hitler's Third Reich, Auden and Isherwood disappeared to America. I wanted to ask them about this, and perhaps it's a great weakness in me that I didn't. But using television to humiliate people publicly is something I find distasteful. Indeed, in our private conversations I did talk about it, but to put a question like that in a live television studio was to open up old wounds, and I knew this one must have been the torment of their lives.

Retreats

Monks, or nuns, are not parasites. To have some people in a society, particularly in an intensely materialistic society like ours, living in that way is absolutely the salt that gives society its savour.

A Hard Bed to Lie On

A visit to the Cistercian monks of Nunraw in Scotland.
They received a special dispensation to break their rule
of silence for this programme

It's half past three in the morning when, for Cistercian monks, the day begins with private devotions and then the Mass. I, too, attend the Mass, kneeling at the back; an outsider. To me it means nothing beyond the spectacle of devout men, the pleasant sound of plainsong. To the monks it is everything – the pivot of their lives, a daily spiritual feast compensating them for the austerities and privations of their strict Cistercian Rule. Are they wasting their time? There are many today who think so. Prayers don't show in the Gross National Product – so why pray? The monks have an answer: the Mass brings them, they say, spiritual nourishment – the body and blood of Christ to swallow ravenously.

Could I ever have been a monk, I ask myself. I can see the attraction of the life – dying in the flesh to be reborn in the spirit. Marvellous! No newspapers, no telly – what joy! But living in a dormitory – communal life and all the little irritations and peculiarities it generates! That I should find tough. Young men still come forward to take it on. Will there be enough of them to fill the large new Abbey high up on a hill which the monks have built to move to from their present old army huts and Victorian mansion?

At meals the Cistercian rule of silence applies at its strictest. The food is still plain and monotonous, but not as meagre as it once was. Nowadays, the monks have cheese, but still no meat or fish or eggs. It all somehow reminds me a little of army life – with the refectory a kind of holy, silent NAAFI.

After Mass and breakfast – in the fields. The monks farm a thousand and more acres, and pride themselves on being

ST. MUG

BY Trog 1966 A.D.

'Could I ever have been a monk?'

Coco Chanel.

P. G. Wodehouse in 1928.

As Editor of Punch 'Humour is the only thing about which the English are completely serious.'

good farmers. After all, they've been at it for some ten centuries. It's part of their rule thus to provide by their own labour for their own needs; not to be a burden on others. Yet some of the younger monks feel that their old-fashioned farming is too remote from today's technological world. They'd sooner work in factories. The twentieth century with all its unresolved doubts and conflicts has somehow penetrated even this enclosed order. The Bishop of Woolwich, as it were, has got into the woodwork; Teillard de Chardin, Paul Tillich are scuttling about under the floorboards. The older monks stick to their rule and Thomas Aquinas.

The new Abbey is nearly finished. It's on any showing an heroic effort, the culmination of twenty years of effort and work by the monks. The design by Peter Whiston is based on Citeau where St Bernard's great Ministry began. How proud he would have been to know that after a thousand years yet another Abbey would be built and occupied in a distant land. Next year the monks will move in – a great day for all of them but also not without its questionings.

MUGGERIDGE: You look very young, Brother Martin. How long have you been a monk?

MARTIN: I've been here about six and a half years.

MUGGERIDGE: So you can take your solemn vows quite soon.

MARTIN: I've taken my solemn vows.

MUGGERIDGE: I see, but not your lifelong vows.

MARTIN: Yes, solemn vows are lifelong vows. Simple profession is just temporary vows.

MUGGERIDGE: So you are a Cistercian monk for life. Presumably you have deliberated long and weighed the matter up and prayed over it and so on?

MARTIN: Well, that's an odd question, because I think for some men they do have a lot of thinking to do and questions to ask, but I found with myself that once I had decided to go on, long before the six months' probationary period was up, I had no more worries at all.

MUGGERIDGE: Marvellous!

MARTIN: That was my experience, not others'.

MUGGERIDGE: It's a difficult life, Brother Martin, isn't it?

MARTIN: Spartan. I suppose that some of the things that we put up with might put other people off; the monotonous round that we have, the very simple food we have; the fact that we never, or rarely, get out anywhere. Other people can always go to the cinema or the theatre . . .

MUGGERIDGE: But you can't.

MARTIN: We don't have anything like that, no.

MUGGERIDGE: Each day is like the one before.

MARTIN: And so much so that one doesn't always know what day it is.

MUGGERIDGE: You don't read daily newspapers?

MARTIN: No.

MUGGERIDGE: I should regard that as one of the great benefits of being monk. That is one of the things that would attract me most. But there's a movement for having newspapers, isn't there?

MARTIN: A lot of us feel that our lack of political knowledge is a hindrance to possibly living this life as we want to live it.

MUGGERIDGE: Would that be a difference between you younger monks and the older ones?

MARTIN: Well, that's hard to say. It may just be a sign of one's youthfulness. I don't know what I will think about it in ten years' time.

MUGGERIDGE: Is there a rift, Brother Martin, of any kind between the younger monks and the older monks? I mean a different attitude towards your way of life?

MARTIN: Well now, sometimes I think there is and sometimes I don't think there is. I certainly feel that the pressures of modern life give us a different outlook on the Cistercian life.

MUGGERIDGE: Different, you mean, from the older monks?

MARTIN: I think so, yes. And it takes time for us to appreciate their viewpoint. What may well change is that we have been up to now – and still are in this monastery – predominantly an agricultural organisation. Our history is wrapped up in agriculture through the centuries. But it may be that monks may think in the future that they ought to move away from the agricultural world into a closer relationship with the people in the cities.

MUGGERIDGE: How long have you been a monk, Brother Oliver?

OLIVER: Well, I entered Rosscrae in 1934, that's in Rosscrae, of course, in Tipperary, and I was there up until I came to Scotland in 1946.

MUGGERIDGE: When you are doing all this outdoor work on the farm, aren't you sometimes hungry?

OLIVER: Yes, you sometimes come home tired. And although the bed is a hard one, you know the old saying that the Cistercian bed is hard to lie on, but it's sweet to die on.

MUGGERIDGE: And you found it a bed hard to lie on?

OLIVER: Oh, indeed I always have done, and to this day I do. That's the one consolation you get when you go to a hospital – you get a lovely soft bed. You can sleep and sleep, and the last time I was in hospital the sister there said she thought I was never going to waken. She said I slept for six days without break – so there you are. That is a fact!

MUGGERIDGE: But sweet to die on?

OLIVER: Yes, it is sweet to die on. Well, that's the reward of a monk's life. I suppose he comes into the monastery to die, or to learn how to die perhaps.

MUGGERIDGE: Is that what you see as the purpose of living in a monastery – to learn how to die?

OLIVER: I think it is – now that's my purpose. I don't say it's everybody's perhaps, but if I didn't think I was going to get to heaven I wouldn't be here three days!

MUGGERIDGE: Why the Cistercians, Father Hugh?

HUGH: Because of the balance of the life. As you have seen,

our life is spread out between three activities, divine office and choir, the reading or *Lexio Divina*, and the manual work. It gives a balanced day and a balanced background for a life of prayer.

MUGGERIDGE: As I understand, a lot of changes have either happened or are pending in the Cistercian rule. Do you think all this is in the right direction?

HUGH: If a living being cannot adapt itself to different conditions, the new conditions will overwhelm it and it will die. We must be men of our day. For instance, I don't think fasting plays quite the same part as it did in a former era. I would say that the pain in the neck today is for the old to put up with the young and the young to put up with the old.

MUGGERIDGE: You mean that would be the real mortification of the flesh?

HUGH: I would say the real mortification of the flesh is the brush of temperament in a life like ours. I don't think it's the physical austerity, I don't think it's the hard beds. You can get used to that. But things like the brush of temperament is something very much harder.

MUGGERIDGE: When you say the brush of temperament, what you mean is people, monks getting on each other's nerves in the nearness of their lives. Is that right?

HUGH: Well, what I mean is things like having a monk next to you in choir who sings habitually flat. It can be very trying, you see. We wouldn't have you in.

MUGGERIDGE: No, I'm sure you wouldn't. I wouldn't even apply to sing in your choir, because I listen to you holding forth like – a singing bird.

Father Abbot, have all the changes made it more difficult to be an Abbot?

ABBOT: Yes, it has because, whereas you could appeal to or lay down the law before and that finished it, now you have to decide each individual case, weigh things up to meet the temperament and individuality of the man.

MUGGERIDGE: So it's more complicated – but easier to

execute?

ABBOT: It's just as if a traffic constable was no longer the law undisputed but could argue with every driver – where he was to go and how he was to turn and who was to go first.

MUGGERIDGE: If that's the image, then I think your job is very tough indeed!

It's half past seven in the evening. For the monks it's the end of another day; their work's over, with only the last office, Compline – to me the loveliest of all – to be sung, then bed. So their days pass, in prayer, work and study; each exactly like the other, the weeks and the months and the years passing and taking them, as the older monks like Brother Oliver confidently believe, nearer to Heaven, or as the younger ones ardently hope, along some path of special illumination.

Will there be enough new vocations to make up their numbers? It's asking a tremendous lot in this age of affluence and materialism to ask a young man to accept this austere disciplined way of life. Whatever may happen to the Cistercians, to the church, or even to Christianity itself, I'm quite sure of one thing: there'll always be a demand among human beings for some to withdraw from the pursuit of fame and money and power and sexual satisfaction and all these other things to which men dedicate their lives, and seek some special relationship with their Creator. And that's what the monks here have tried to do, and the efforts they've made won't be lost.

Political Honours

After the Prime Minister's statement about Honours, throughout the Home Counties and beyond massive ladies in tweed suits and gardening gloves have been heard openly sobbing over their rose beds, and Lt Colonels with trimmed

white moustaches groaning and howling as they mowed their lawns within sight of Sevenoaks station. No more OBE's and MBE's for party political services in the annual Queen's Birthday and New Year hand-outs. A cruel blow indeed!

There was a time not so very long ago in the good old

Lloyd George days when honours and peerages were on free sale. A barony cost £40,000. A Viscountcy rather more – up to £100,000 – though, if Lord Beaverbrook is to be believed, Lord Astor paid twice that sum for his. And a knighthood could be picked up for as little as £10,000. A middle man in the business named Maundy Gregory got caught out and had to be prosecuted. After serving a short sentence he decamped to Paris where he lived quietly as Sir Arthur Gregory. It showed a becoming modesty on his part. There was, after all, nothing to stop him giving himself a peerage. When he ran short of money he just used to send postcards to former clients announcing his intention of returning to London. Cheques came rolling by return of post.

A favourite anecdote of Gregory's was of a client who signed a cheque in payment for a peerage with the title he proposed to take, thus ensuring that there would be no double-dealing. Another case that he liked to dwell on was of an aspiring nobleman who paid for his peerage on the instalment plan and died before the payments were completed, thereby creating a problem for his heirs.

After Gregory a committee was set up to ensure that thenceforth peerages and other honours should be disinterestedly bestowed. This did not preclude the ennoblement of Lord Thomson of Fleet, who, according to his biographer, Russell Braddon, sent his naturalisation papers to the office of the then Prime Minister, Mr Macmillan, marked 'For Attention'. He received them back marked 'Duly Noted', and was awarded his peerage in the next Honours List.

It seems extraordinary, in a way, that any sane citizen should still want to become a lord or a member of an Order named after an empire which no longer exists. Yet, as any Prime Minister's postbag clearly indicates, the appetite remains undiminished. This has its advantages. Honours and decorations cost nothing; if their recipients had to be bribed to keep in line it would become expensive. An American President, groaning over the spoils system, would be only too glad to have a few peerages and knighthoods to bestow. Dryden's line on a politician of the day – 'For almonds he'll cry whore to his own mother' – remains apposite if for almonds we read MBE's.

Air Hostesses
If a woman is pretty and she smiles at me I want to be sure, or my vanity wants to be sure, that she's smiling at me to please me, and if I see a girl smiling at everybody with equal idiot amiability it's irritating.

Air Travel
In an aeroplane one senses the fallacy of travel. The faster and higher they go, the more they seem to stand still.

Paris — 1944

I started off as a private in the war, joining up in 1939 to escape from writing propaganda stories in the Ministry of Information, which was my idea of hell. If God really wants to punish me in eternity, he'll make me do that because it's real torture. Then I became an ordinary regimental Intelligence officer but later was pulled out and put in MI6, the wartime version of the Secret Service, to spend eighteen curious months in Lourenço Marques as a bogus Vice-Consul, staying in the one and only hotel with my opposite numbers – Italian and German – all three of us together, all spying on each other, never of course addressing a word to each other.

I've always thought that news is the most phoney thing there is, but it's relatively factual compared to Intelligence reports, which are usually pure fantasy. There's no check you can put on them. In this last war I was one of the very junior figures in it, but the messages of my opposite number, the German man in Mozambique, Dr Wertz, presented me as a dynamic figure in charge of all Intelligence in Africa, his purpose being to enhance his own importance. Here I am making a monkey of this man and look what an important chap he is! Needless to say, this was by no means the case.

After the Normandy invasion took place, I came to Paris, and for me the war ended in the Boulevard Suchet in a rather nice office overlooking the Bois de Boulogne with very little to do. My job was primarily to act as liaison officer for passing on to British Intelligence anything the French Intelligence wanted to pass on to them, and vice versa. But in practice it was much more to do with looking after people who had worked for us during the occupation as double agents, and who had therefore, of necessity, been on good terms with the occupation authorities. So, from the point of view of ordinary people, they were traitors, and were being arrested and beaten up, and one had to try and protect them. There was also the question – one of the most fascinating aspects of Intelligence work – were they working for us or for the enemy? It was an almost impossible distinction to make. My opinion, for what it was worth, having read a good many of these dossiers and met a certain number of the people concerned, was that double agents, in time, just don't know who they are or what they're supposed to be doing – whether they're supposed to be murdering somebody, sleeping with somebody, or searching through their wastepaper baskets. A state of total confusion. Behind it all was the very simple fact you might miss out unless you studied their dossiers – that if they were Germans their main motive was to stay in Paris, where they could have a pleasant time, rather than go to the Eastern Front where they would have a very uncomfortable time. As the war was nearly over, I just gave them the benefit of the doubt, and decided they were, on the whole, working for us.

Kim Philby was my boss while I was in Mozambique because he looked after Portugal and Spain; and then in Paris he was, strangely enough, put in charge of the anti-Soviet organisation that they were then setting up. In fact, when one read about the Intelligence operations in the war, the glow of victory completely disappeared because, for instance, Admiral Canaris, whom we regarded as our No. 1 target as Head of the German Intelligence, turned out to be on our side. Philby was working for the Soviet Government; who was working for what? At the end of the day it felt rather like having with great difficulty won a football match only to find that the man keeping goal on the other side was letting the balls through – it took away some of the exhilaration of victory!

Philby wasn't a particularly interesting person at the time – only afterwards when one read about it all. I have to admit that I hadn't the slightest suspicion of him as a double agent. In fact, I thought he was booted out of the Secret Service because he had made a fool of himself having Burgess to stay with him. I even tried to help him get a job as a journalist. Something about him that I think is too little understood is the appalling stutter that he had – the worst I've ever known. He would fight to get words out, and it was very difficult to have a serious discussion with him about anything. His agony in getting the words out was so terrible that one would naturally let the matter drop.

I had a very curious evening with him once in Paris – we'd both had too much to drink, and he said let's go to the Rue de Grenelle. I thought it might be some night club that he thought particularly amusing, but it was to stand outside the Soviet Embassy, where he began to bellyache about the terrible difficulty of penetrating it, how everything there was guarded, the impossibility of suborning the servants – almost as though he was out of his mind. Whether he was trying to tell me something, I simply don't know.

For me Maxim's is holy ground because we came to this famous restaurant very soon after arriving in Paris, and to our great satisfaction they refused to give us a bill. The reason was clear: no doubt German officers had been patronising the restaurant a few days before, and it was good to have a few allied officers in to purify it, as it were. It only lasted for two or three days; then the bills began to come, and they were very high. But it was rather glorious up till then to feel you could go to Maxim's and order what you liked free of charge.

There were many people and institutions that were vaguely in trouble when the liberation came. Everybody collaborates with an occupying force: if you had a restaurant you had German officers amongst your clients; if your were a prostitute you slept with German officers; if you were a barber you cut their hair; and if you were an entertainer like Maurice Chevalier you entertained them, so there really was a great deal to worry about. The French refer to it very characteristically as having 'des ennuies' – little troubles, little irritations. I remember even Picasso (whom I met once at the British Embassy when the Duff Coopers were there) was a little bit uneasy because his studio had been warmed during the occupation, and that meant that he had in some degree good relations with the occupying powers. The funniest case I thought was Madame Chanel, who was in difficulties – she had a German friend, and the police didn't like that very much – but she thought of a brilliant idea, rather Napoleonic in its simplicity and directness. She simply put a notice in her shop, *'Chanel No.5 Gratuit aux GI's'* – 'free for GI's'. She never had any more troubles after that.

George Orwell came to Paris as *The Observer* correspondent, dressed in battle dress. He very ardently wanted to get in to the army and fight in the war, but of course his health precluded it, and this was the nearest he got. I never saw any of the stories he did in *The Observer*, but he was some little time in Paris and he used to come ferreting around looking as ever like a fish out of water. He's one of those men who never seems to be quite fitting into his environment. As a war correspondent, equally, he was rather charmingly ill cast.

I loved his writings, and I liked his mind very much and even his eccentricity. His wild statements used to amuse me. For instance, he would suddenly say to you: 'All tobacconists are fascists.' And he was so convincing in a way that you'd think: 'By jove, yes, those little men in those kiosks, I bet they've all got swastikas under their belts.' Then you'd think afterwards. 'This is utterly absurd. There must be tobacconists who are socialists, marxists, liberals,' although I suppose there might be a grain of truth in it. Perhaps sitting in a kiosk passing out tobacco might develop in one the sort of mood out of which fascism comes!

After the liberation, the first time I saw De Gaulle was at Notre Dame Cathedral, when they had a great service of Thanksgiving. The big event was that somebody fired a pistol. Nobody knows why, but it was thought to be trouble because there were heaps of odd fugitive Germans around; there were also the FFI – mostly Communists who'd kept their weapons and were going to have a big try to take over. Plenty of people would have been very happy to fire a shot at the General; and practically everybody in the Cathedral fell flat on the ground except this extraordinary figure standing there. It seemed to symbolise the position of De Gaulle in the country – everybody flat on the ground, muddled. He alone had this peculiar confidence in his own authority which enabled him to take over. Nobody ever authorised him as far as I know, but he just *was* in fact the government, and recognised as such. It's hard to understand whence this authority came. He certainly wasn't a man with charisma – to use our rather rotten contemporary word. He seemed a gauche person, with plenty of enemies in France on the Left and on the Right; but nobody ever questioned his integrity, his personal disinterestedness. In all the rows that he was involved in nobody would ever suggest that he was corrupt in any way, because to do so would have been a waste of time.

He was a great man not so much because of what he did as because of what he was. He had a sense of history: a sense of his country's destiny. Also, compared with the other contemporary politicians – Roosevelt, Churchill, and so on – he was a genuinely religious man. He had a handicapped daughter, a mongol child, and he somehow managed, every day, to spend a little time with her. She died in her early twenties as mongol children often do, and at the funeral when he and his wife were standing by the grave, he made this remark: '*Maintenant elle est comme les autres*,' 'Now she's like the others.' I think it's a very beautiful thing to have said.

One of the many pleasures of old age is that you realise that history is largely rubbish. People write about incidents in which you've been involved, such as this so-called liberation of Paris. You read it, and it bears practically no resemblance to what you remember. It gives the impression that there was an enormous wave of joy – 'We're delivered from the Germans!' In actual fact there was a tremendous scene of confusion, in which many private grievances were worked off. There was no law. Whether the Germans were here or weren't here was beside the point. The French could afterwards, in their own inimitable way, run their own affairs, as they're doing now. That was something. But it wasn't liberation. For me it was a great send up of the whole notion of liberation, intensified by the spectacle of people in distress and under strain, who, to prove their ardour for freedom, hit out at other people. Take the simple example of a girl dragged through the street, her hair shaved because she had slept with a German: there's no liberation there.

But it was something I wouldn't have missed as an experience, because it so illuminated this word – freedom – that has haunted our time. As we have fallen into ever deeper servitude in different ways – either through self-indulgence, or through accepting some ideology which is then imposed and turned into a dictatorship – more and more talk has been heard about freedom. Africa's been liberated, India's been liberated, and you ask yourself what does it really mean in terms of people's lives, to the degree which their lives have become free – that's another thing altogether. To understand it you have to eliminate various phantom liberations. For instance, you can't liberate people by force. The communists have taught that you can. Mao Tse Tung said: freedom lies at the end of a gun. It doesn't: whenever force is used to achieve this ostensible liberation it turns out to be servitude. Nor can you achieve liberation by simply enabling people to do whatever they have a mind to, because that produces our sort of society, in which people are enslaved to their appetites. But behind it all, it is possible for human beings to be free. I personally believe that they can only be free in their relationship to their Creator, in their awareness of what human life is really about. Loving someone else more than yourself, that's freedom. That's what Solzhenitsyn came to understand in the Gulag – that they were captives in ghastly conditions, but they were free because, through their circumstances, they'd understood what it meant to be free.

You would look in vain for anything that could possibly be called liberation in any true sense of the word in what happened in Paris in 1944. The Germans couldn't stay and went. The Allies moved in. The French cheered with a good many reservations. It used to make me laugh when, in the last resort, they might say to you when something was going on of which they very much disapproved: 'You know that would never have happened when the Germans were here.' The mere shifting of power isn't freedom. Put down the mighty from their seats and exalt the humble and meek, but what happens to the humble and the meek when they're exalted? They, too, have to be put down. It's an endless process, but a man's freedom is only achieved through his own vision of reality – and that must lie in a mystical rather than an historical truth.

BS

When Graham Greene and I were first put into MI6 and trained, in a manner of speaking, for being spies, it involved learning how to write in invisible inks. One substance to be used in extremis *was called BS, which means bird shit. The idea was to collect it, dissolve it in water and use it as invisible ink. It's not as easy as you might think to procure supplies but luckily I was never reduced to that extreme condition.*

The English aren't a particularly militaristic people – when they go to war they always go with the last war in mind. And I think that secret ink belonged to the 1914-18 war more than the 1939-45 one.

Virgin Birth

It would have been attractive on many occasions in one's rather murky past if one could have put forward this theory with assurance.

Dying

I'm very content that I'm going to die soon because that is part of the process of living.

To Die like an Angel

MUGGERIDGE: Mother Teresa and her Sisters of Charity live in one of Calcutta's poorest slums. It's a natural place for them to be. In addition to the traditional vows of poverty, chastity and obedience, the Sisters take one of dedication to the service of the poorest of the poor. Each day begins for them at 4.30 in the morning, with mass in their chapel. After mass and breakfast they do the washing and other household chores. The buckets they use represent, along with two white saris, the sum total of their worldly possessions.

The noises of the street outside endlessly intrude, which is considered by Mother Teresa to be appropriate to their work and circumstances.

MOTHER TERESA: I wanted to be a missionary, to go out and give the life of Christ to the people in the missionary countries. Some missionaries had come to India from Yugoslavia and they told me of the Loreto nuns who were doing work in Calcutta and other places. I offered myself to the Bengal mission and from there they sent me to India, in 1929.

MUGGERIDGE: Mother Teresa, when did the feeling that you must dedicate yourself to the poor people come to you?

MOTHER TERESA: It was many years ago when I was at home with my people in Skopje in Yugoslavia. I was only twelve years old then. It was like a vocation that Christ chooses. In 1931 I took my first vows in Loreto. Then in 1937 I took my final vows there.

MUGGERIDGE: Between the age of twelve and that time did you have any doubts, any hesitations about taking on this way of life?

MOTHER TERESA: At the beginning, between twelve and eighteen, I didn't want to become a nun. We were a very happy family. But at eighteen I decided to leave home and since then, these forty years, I've never doubted even for a second that I've done the right thing. It was the will of God; it was His choice.

MUGGERIDGE: And this has given you complete serenity, peace and happiness?

MOTHER TERESA: A happiness that no one can take from me. There has never been a doubt or unhappiness.

MUGGERIDGE: And then you became aware of certain circumstances in the world outside.

MOTHER TERESA: It was a second calling. A vocation to give up even Loreto, where I was very happy, and to go out in the streets to serve the poorest of the poor.

MUGGERIDGE: You must have had some money presumably. Where did that come from?

MOTHER TERESA: At first I had only five rupees. And gradually – as people came to know what I was doing, they brought money and things. It was all divine providence because right from the very first I didn't ask for any money.

MUGGERIDGE: The money had to be voluntary contributions?

MOTHER TERESA: It was all a gift. From the very beginning, I wanted to serve the poor purely for the love of God – what the rich people get with money I wanted to give to the poor for the love of God.

MUGGERIDGE: What was the next move?

MOTHER TERESA: The sisters started coming. The first sister that joined our congregation was Sister Agnes in 1949. She's my assistant now.

MUGGERIDGE: She was a girl in Loreto, wasn't she?

MOTHER TERESA: She was a schoolgirl in Loreto. The first ten girls were all students that I had taught in the school. With them others came to help us on a voluntary basis – doctors, nurses, and in 1952 we opened the first Home for the Dying.

MUGGERIDGE: These are people, I take it, who are abandoned and dying in the streets?

MOTHER TERESA: Yes. The first woman that I saw I myself

217

picked up from the street. She had been half-eaten by rats and ants. I took her to the hospital and they accepted her because I refused to move from there until they took her in. From there, I went to the municipality and I asked them just to give me a place where I could bring these people, because on the same day I found more people dying in the streets. The health officer took me to the Kali temple. It was an empty building, so he asked me if I would accept that. Within twenty-four hours we had our patient there and started the work for the sick and dying destitutes. And since then we have picked up over 23,000 people from the streets of Calcutta, of which about half have died.

MUGGERIDGE: Mother Teresa, a lot of people who see these poor castaways in here are going to say to themselves: what's the point of trying to keep them alive, protracting a little longer such sad lives?

MOTHER TERESA: Well, in these twenty years of work amongst the people, I have more and more realised that being unwanted is the worst disease that the human being can ever experience. Because nowadays we have found medicine for leprosy and they can be cured. There is medicine for TB, they can be cured. But for being unwanted – except for willing hands to serve them and a loving heart to love them – I don't think that terrible disease can ever be cured.

MUGGERIDGE: And it's that disease that you're looking after.

MOTHER TERESA: We want to make them feel that at the end somebody loves and cares for them. That's why we want to give them the best of what they have missed right through their lives. As somebody said, they have lived like animals but now they die like angels.

MUGGERIDGE: And that is what you feel really is your job when they come here?

MOTHER TERESA: To help them to die like angels.

MUGGERIDGE: You said you also worked with lepers.

MOTHER TERESA: Yes, we have over 9000 lepers that we are treating in Calcutta itself, with a mobile clinic. And the specially trained sisters go to those centres and people from all over that area come for this treatment which we have up to date. Thank God we have been able to save many people by curing them completely. And the most wonderful part that has happened, though it sounds terrible to say it, but the increase of numbers is a very good sign for us.

MUGGERIDGE: Why is that?

MOTHER TERESA: Because before they used to hide their disease, and when it's very far gone you can do very little for it. But now we get very young cases which in a year or two can be completely cured. So we are very happy that our numbers are growing. That's a sign that the people are beginning to be conscious of all the disease, and of wanting to be all right. Also we actually go to them; they don't have to come in public. And when they see our young sisters going amongst them with so much love and care for them, they begin to feel that confidence, and are not afraid to come and tell. Because in India leprosy is a disease that they are ashamed and afraid of. Once a leper, a man's a leper for life, and he will lose his job and lose everything in life. He may even lose his family. So when they see the sisters coming amongst them, that encourages them to come forward, to bring their family and have them all examined and treated.

MUGGERIDGE: Even in this short visit I've sensed, as I never have before, that these lepers and these little children that you get off the street aren't just destitute people to be pitied, but marvellous people. That's the extraordinary thing that you do. Anybody who has enough can pity someone who hasn't enough. Anybody who's well can pity a man who's sick. But I think what you do is to make one see that they're not *just* to be pitied; they are marvellous people. Now how do you do this?

MOTHER TERESA: We do it *to* God, *to* Christ, and that's why we try to do it as beautifully as possible, because it is continual contact with Christ in His poor, as we have during Mass and in the Blessed Sacrament. But here in the slums, in the broken bones in the children, we see Christ and we touch Him. And that touch comes from the deep faith in Christ.

MUGGERIDGE: That's almost your favourite word, 'beautiful', isn't it? Even when we asked you to do this programme – you were reluctant to do it – you said, 'Well let's do something beautiful for God'. Whether we have or not I don't know, but I'm quite sure you are doing things that are beautiful. You see, Mother, I think that twentieth-century man is so made that he always thinks there must be a collective solution to everything. When he looks at what you're doing he thinks, 'It's superb. But it's nothing. There ought to be some big practical way of doing this.' His feeling about that makes him less inclined to throw himself in the way that you want into the sort of work that you're doing. Do you agree with that?

MOTHER TERESA: Well, I do not agree with that big way of doing things, because to us what matters is the individual; to get to love the person we must come in close contact with him. If we wait till we get the numbers, then we will be lost in the numbers. And we will never be able to show that love and respect for the person. I believe in person to person. Every person is Christ for me and that's why, since there is only one Jesus, then that person is the only person for me at that moment.

MUGGERIDGE: Yes, I'm sure that's right, but the difficulty that I see is how to make people whose minds have been formed in the circumstances of today realise this. Even the churches – though this is the gospel on which they're based – fail to inculcate this particular feeling of person to person.

MOTHER TERESA: The people of today think the poor are not like human beings. They look down on them. But if they had that deep respect for the dignity of poor people, I'm sure it would be easy for them to come closer to them, and feel that they too are the children of God, and that they have as much right to the things of life and of love and of service as anybody else. But in these times of development we are much too busy; everybody is in a hurry and a rush, and on the way there are always people falling to both sides who are not able. These are the ones that we want to love, serve, take up and take care of.

MUGGERIDGE: And do with them beautiful things for God.

Nobel Prize
Strange to think Mother Teresa wins a Peace Prize provided by the inventor of dynamite!

Opinion Polls
Totally fraudulent! I much prefer the method of the ancient Romans – they used to throw the entrails of a chicken on the ground, and from the way they fell deduce the future. The only modification I'd suggest would be to use, instead of the entrails of a chicken, why not Dr Gallup's entrails, even though they could only be used once?

Politicians
American politicians are said to be corrupt, and English politicians honest. This is true. I like Stephen Leacock's comment on the observation – 'American politicians will do anything for money, English politicians take the money and won't do anything.'

Ideal Government
A broken-down democracy in a time of economic crisis, for me temperamentally, is a perfect state of affairs; being so ramshackle and run down, it is unable to interfere seriously with the things that I delight in. A society in disarray provides, for those with an anarchic temperament and their wits about them, a rather agreeable situation.

From Our Own
Correspondent: Washington

In 1946, just after I had been demobilised, I reached the conclusion that Washington had become the centre of the world. I had felt just the same in 1932 about Moscow. Now I wanted to go to Washington, which I duly managed to do, this time as correspondent for *The Daily Telegraph*. I stayed there for two years. It really was the centre of the world I found, but, oh God, what a world! I left with relief, and then last year I went back for the first time in twenty years to have another look around. The same old honeypot of news, the same swarms of newsgatherers buzzing round it. I've got no buzz left in me now and am well content to sit in my Sussex garden. But in Washington last year I found the buzz louder than ever.

The city still exists after all, grown larger, visibly swollen with its own importance. It never has had anything to do with America. Just a seat of government, a rainbow in the wide sky of American power and wealth at whose end all mankind are digging for crocks of gold. What's been happening in my absence? What has the wild tickertape been saying? The truth is that news, like beauty, is in the eye of the beholder. If all the newsgatherers and all the rotary presses and all the teleprinters and all the television cameras were silenced, shut up, there wouldn't be any news. But if you took all the newsgatherers and their gear and put them in the middle of the Sahara, or in the stratosphere, there'd be more news than ever. News in the newsgatherers' sense bears the same relation to events as muzak does to music.

Journalism, too, is tremendously a matter of taking in each other's washing. We could generally find something in one of the American papers, coming from London, to be sent back there like a wonderful transatlantic game of tennis.

James Reston in Washington picks up a story from London, dishes it up as from 'State Department sources', or 'informed circles in the White House', and bashes it back to London. In London they pick it up, and back it comes to Washington, where you are waiting for it at the net to smash it down – fifteen all!

In the National Press Building, in each office and cubicle the same scene is being enacted, the same tickertape's churning out the same words, to be scrutinised by different eyes looking for different treasure. A news broiler house kept at an even temperature, identical lighting and food for all, but each of us expected to lay his own personalised eggs in the shape of exclusive stories, fashioned and angled for our particular readers. Our own correspondent's very own egg. Unfertilised, of course.

Inevitably, in Washington, my steps frequently led me to the White House, 1600 Pennsylvania Avenue, a residence not a place; the house of the Common Man in the century of the Common Man. Who governs America? It was a question I often put to myself in my newsgathering days in Washington without ever finding a wholly satisfying answer. In the Cabinet Room of the White House what passes for being the government meets and deliberates; the President seated in his own special chair – in my day, Harry Truman, still not quite used to the authority which had so unexpectedly fallen on him, as he put it, 'out of the sky'. Seated at a long table, little, little men. Shall we, shan't we? Shall we what? Blow the earth and all mankind to smithereens. In my mind's eye, I filled the chairs, listened to the discussions. Perhaps after all that's how the world does end – with little men seated at a table.

I myself always had a special fancy for the minor ceremonial occasion – for instance, the unveiling of a portrait of Mrs Truman by the reigning First Lady, Mrs Ladybird Johnson. We newsgatherers had our part on such occasions, a walking-on part – pencil, microphone or camera in hand – acolytes all. I'd always turn up for a non-story, enjoying the spectacle of obsequiousness for obsequiousness's own sake. Pictures taken, and notes scribbled, without any expectation of their making news. My Ladybird, my Texan Jacky! – 'Friends, this is a very happy occasion for me. For a long time I've felt that the White House should have a portrait of Mrs Truman . . .'

Dear Bess Truman, I liked her better in her homely person than in her portrait. We're all poor players – but still with lines to say, exits to make, parts to perform – as in the case of First Ladies – parts wholly devised and presented by public relations men. No longer any need to strive to be sincere as a human being. Just devise, or pick up an image provided by public relations staff, and try to live up to it. If the image gets damaged, it's almost like blasphemy in the medieval church.

Considering past Presidents in this light, Thomas Jefferson, the most brilliant President, had a bad habit of staring, and he wouldn't have been good on television. And Abraham Lincoln wouldn't have gone over too well either because, frankly, he had ugly features that wouldn't show up very well – not to mention very eccentric ways – and a bad twang – a little like the man from Texas. On consideration, it seems that the only two Presidents who could really have done extremely well would have been Warren Harding and Franklin Pierce – regarded as the two worst Presidents ever.

The State Department, after the White House, was our most frequent port of call. In my day it was in the old Executive Building, adjoining the White House; now in its own byzantine quarters, erected on what used to be a marsh known as Foggy Bottom – a weird blend of the old and the new worlds, like one of the marriages American heiresses used to make with European princelings. It might almost be Monaco with its elegance, its period pieces languishing outside all periods; the Fragonard, for instance, mock or real – who knows or for that matter cares – looking down on dinner parties whose tedium lingers on like dust on the polished floor!

We newsgatherers had to try and extract nourishment in the shape of news out of the marble halls. It was hard going then, and has not, I note, got any easier. In Washington I was my own legman. Not so easy in America where pedestrians are suspect, and traffic rules all. I used to think of my passage from one government department to another – State, Commerce, Treasury, Interior – like the Stations of the Cross, pausing at each one to beat my breast and mutter, 'Mea Culpa! Give us this day our daily story'; then on to the next. Up Massachusetts Avenue where all the embassies are; a long haul to the British Embassy where there are also stories to be picked up, and public relations men like radar screens ensuring that one lands at one's allotted berth. 'Anything cooking, old boy?' From one old boy to another old boy, with sometimes, as a special treat, admission to a real diplomat, who knew real secrets. In my time, ironically enough, this usually turned out to be Donald Maclean.

I always think of Washington as a sort of Turkish bath – and not just because it's often hot and steamy and soporific. Once, feeling in need of reparation, I had a real Turkish bath at an establishment long since defunct, called rather unappetisingly, if I remember correctly, Ringworm Hall. The apparatus was extremely antique, and indeed seemed almost to be falling to pieces. Nonetheless the place had considerable social cachet, and when I came to and began to peer through the steam I saw quite near me the familiar features of none other than the then British Ambassador, Lord Inverchapel, a curious figure with a rather large nose, and naturally very rubicund – of course, in these circumstances more so than ever. As I'd just been warned off the British Embassy for being what's called 'unhelpful' – which means, in the trade, letting someone else's cat out of your bag – I thought it best to divert my eyes – exchanging a wink, however, with his private secretary, who was being steamed beside him, presumably to be on hand if some prescient thought or remark was steamed out of His Excellency. It all seemed, somehow, very symbolic of this federal capital whose only industry is government, and whose only output is words. Words ceaselessly produced, like steam, and then distilled into heavy drops of information, which in turn are evaporated again into steam.

The Pentagon was the most awesome of all my Stations of

the Cross, a whole world apart; self-contained and self-sufficient, with its own built-in tutorial system, and even tricycles for the messengers distributing documents and occasionally for visitors like me. One might pedal along its interminable corridors for ever without getting anywhere or meeting anyone. In fact, they lead nowhere, have no beginning, no end. Can it be, I used to wonder, that the greatest war potential in history resolves itself into corridors along which one can bike for hours on end. The Supreme Headquarters where allegedly a button can be touched and lo! no world, no us. I say, anyone in? Where's General Mars, Admiral Neptune, Staff Captain Prometheus? 'Trouble with his liver at the moment, I daresay.' At last I find something –

227

news, lashings and lashings of it, an enormous cache of handouts of one sort or another, all most secret and saying nothing at all.

Abraham Lincoln in his memorial looked down on the federal capital he so valiantly preserved for posterity – what does he make of it now? So vast a concentration of wealth and power, with behind it so infirm a purpose. I, too, as a newsgatherer, a little satellite riding through its stratosphere – looking down – trying to find a mainspring, the driving force. Not, surely, in the stale rhetoric hanging like a cloud over Capitol Hill? Nor in the White House's tired, dispirited tenants? Nor in the Treasury's paper treasure, nor in the Pentagon's Generals waiting for orders? No guiding light in the briefings and handouts so plentifully provided. Where then? Or has your Union, dear Abe, turned into a fantasy, an American dream indeed from which we shall all, perhaps soon, have to awaken?

Watergate
The unrestrained use of television ultimately makes government impossible, as the Watergate affair is dramatically illustrating.

Hot Line
The proceedings of the Australian Federal Parliament are a wonderful sight at 7.30 in the evening when Honourable Members gather round the microphones and shout messages to their constituents, some of which – believe me – are far from complimentary!

Facts
If I was a praying man, which unfortunately I'm not, I should pray to be delivered from facts, and I'm sure that when our civilisation finally sinks, and the waves close over its head, it will be because it's stuffed, stupefied with facts.

Actors
Politicians are actors who play themselves.

Paul: Envoy Extraordinary

In his footsteps

The famous cathedral at the very heart of London is named after Paul, 'a servant of Jesus Christ, chosen to be an Apostle', as he begins his incomparable letter to the Romans. He was born in Tarsus in southern Turkey at the beginning of the Christian era, the son of a strict orthodox Jew who was also a Roman citizen. As he said himself, a Hebrew of the Hebrews, a hater and persecutor of Christians until on the Damascus road he saw a bright light whose illumination reached far beyond the Law and the Scriptures. Thenceforth until his death, probably in Rome round about AD 67, he carried the gospel of Christ to the pagan world, in the process building up a church which survives to this day and a great civilisation – ours. So with my old friend Alec Vidler we follow him along the way he went, taking account of his letters to the Christian congregations, so vividly, so humanly, so beautifully expressed, and we may look back across the centuries and hope to know the kind of man he was and the work he did.

MUGGERIDGE: I must say it's a funny chance, Alec, if one looks back to fifty years ago when we were undergraduates together, that we should be standing in Tarsus looking for St Paul. During that fifty years not only have you been my dearest and oldest friend, but you have also been studying the New Testament, the Epistles – you're a theologian, an expert. I can't claim any of that. But in a way that has a certain advantage, because at least I shall come freshly to exploring these extraordinary documents which I'm quite convinced on any showing are among the most luminous ever written in the history of the world.

VIDLER: Well, I agree. For both of us I take it, after Jesus, Paul is the key figure in the whole Christian story.

★   ★   ★

MUGGERIDGE: Some time after Stephen's martyrdom Paul took the road to Damascus, which leads by Galilee. His purpose in going there was to ferret out any of the Jews who seemed to be influenced by Christian teaching. It seems to me that he was the most insatiable persecutor.

VIDLER: Yes, indeed, but this doesn't surprise me because after all he was a man of fiery temperament.

MUGGERIDGE: It was on the road that the great decisive experience of his life so mysteriously took place. I believe there are three accounts of it in the Acts, aren't there?

VIDLER: Yes, yes. And I'll read the one I think is best, shall I? 'So I journeyed to Damascus with the authority and commission of the chief priests. At midday I saw on the way a light from heaven, brighter than the sun, shining round about me and those who journeyed with me. And when we'd all fallen to the ground I heard a voice saying to me in the Hebrew language "Saul, Saul, why do you persecute me? I am Jesus whom you are persecuting. But rise, stand upon your feet, for I've appeared to you to deliver you from the people and from the Gentiles to whom I send you to open their eyes that they may turn from darkness to light."'

MUGGERIDGE: Conversion is something that you as a priest must have met with often. Like Paul, a person being reborn, becoming a new man.

VIDLER: Yes indeed, and it seemed quite sudden. But of course sudden conversions are seldom as sudden as they seem. I remember reading somewhere that our twentieth-century psychologist Jung has remarked that Paul had been a Christian long before his conversion, but unconsciously.

MUGGERIDGE: You mean fighting against something that he knew would ultimately captivate and capture him?

VIDLER: Yes. He added that fanaticism of the kind Paul had been displaying is nearly always a compensation for secret doubt.

MUGGERIDGE: After Paul's extraordinary experience on the Damascus road, he naturally wanted to get away and be alone. In the Acts of the Apostles it says to Arabia. That means to the desert – quiet, solitude.

★　　★　　★

MUGGERIDGE: Perga, obviously the ruins of a majestic city.

VIDLER: Yes, on this occasion in their journeyings Paul and his companions don't seem to have stopped, though on a later visit they would preach here. The only thing we're told happened on this occasion is that John Mark left them.

MUGGERIDGE: There was a row I gather.

VIDLER: Certainly. The reason is not clear. Various guesses have been made; one is that he didn't at all like the idea of a journey up into the mountains, bandit-infested and dangerous; another is that he was simply a young man who was homesick and wanted to get back to Jerusalem where his mother lived. But I think a more likely reason is that at this time Mark's sympathies about the Christian mission were with Peter and the Jewish Christians in Jerusalem, rather than with Paul, and so in a way he parted on a matter of principle.

MUGGERIDGE: You don't think that people found it difficult to get on with Paul?

VIDLER: No, I don't. He had an extraordinary power of gripping the affections and faithfulness of his colleagues and associates, both young and old, and this I regard as a quite exceptional incident.

MUGGERIDGE: He was a very masterful person, Alec, wasn't he?

VIDLER: Oh indeed. And very impulsive. I personally would have found him rather difficult, but those who worked with him, apart from Mark and afterwards Barnabus who left over this same matter, all got on well with him, I think.

MUGGERIDGE: I suppose it is possible that just because Mark and Barnabus belonged to what one could call without irreverence the old gang, it was more difficult for them than for later comers to accept Paul's dominant leadership.

VIDLER: This may well be so.

MUGGERIDGE: Anyway, he took on this journey into these wild places to visit the cities there. Why do you think he did it?

VIDLER: It has been suggested that he had an attack of malaria here and wanted to get up into the high country.

MUGGERIDGE: It's complete bosh, isn't it? I've had malaria myself and I know that wouldn't be plausible.

VIDLER: No, though he does say he first preached up in those cities in the interior because of an 'infirmity of the flesh'. I myself think it was probably some nervous disorder that gave him splitting headaches and migraines, affecting his sight and speech sometimes. This seems to account for most of the references to it.

MUGGERIDGE: People tend to credit a person with their own infirmities, as I do. I've always thought that he must have been an insomniac. Reading the Epistles one can see quite clearly that he had what we'd call today a manic-depressive temperament – his moods alternated violently: he'd be extremely cheerful and very depressed, extremely satirical and sharp, and very loving towards people. What did he look like, Alec?

VIDLER: Well, it's a nice question. While we've no absolutely authentic and reliable testimony there is a passage that seems to have the ring of authenticity about it: I wonder what you'll think. 'Paul, a man of small stature with his eyebrows meeting and a rather large nose, somewhat bald-headed and bandy-legged, strongly built, of gracious presence, for sometimes he looked like a man and sometimes he had the face of an angel.'

MUGGERIDGE: That's a terrific piece, Alec. I would say that's almost sure to be true; you couldn't invent so vivid and lifelike a description.

★   ★   ★

MUGGERIDGE: As Paul and Barnabus continued their journey inland they must have passed by Lake Eğridir, mustn't they?

And, I imagine, paused to admire the marvellous scenery.

VIDLER: My dear Malcolm, when did Paul ever admire any natural scenery?

MUGGERIDGE: That's true enough. He wasn't a lover of nature, was he?

VIDLER: No. I think this derives from his Jewish background. There's very little appreciation in the Old Testament of natural beauty. There are the Psalms, but on the whole the Jews were suspicious of natural beauty because it was associated with paganism and idolatry.

MUGGERIDGE: Do you think this only came in with Wordsworth?

VIDLER: I wouldn't go so far as that, but nature mysticism, as we know it now, does largely derive from him, yes.

MUGGERIDGE: But strangely enough Jesus himself used many most beautiful images taken from the Lake and from natural scenes of every kind.

VIDLER: Indeed, this is very, very striking. But Paul took his images from urban life. He was a townsman.

MUGGERIDGE: And a rather gregarious man. Apart from that time in Arabia he never seems to have been alone; he wasn't that sort of mystic, was he? He enjoyed human company, and his mysticism was directed towards God.

VIDLER: Yes certainly, and towards Christ and mankind as recreated in Christ.

MUGGERIDGE: But not with this sense of oneness in the natural universe. So we see him walking by Lake Eğridir not particularly preoccupied by the lake or the mountains.

VIDLER: I fear that is so. It may be partly because he was shortsighted.

★　★　★

MUGGERIDGE: You know, Alec, one of the reasons I love travelling round this part of the world with you is that it reinforces my contempt for history. All this past obliterated, but not St Paul's words.

VIDLER: Well, that's not very flattering to me! I wouldn't speak so contemptuously of history, being a bit of an historian myself. It reminds me of Paul's words: 'The things that are seen are transient or temporal, the things that are unseen are eternal', which is a much better thing to say.

MUGGERIDGE: That's what I was trying to say.

VIDLER: Ah well, I'm very glad you should say it in a better way.

MUGGERIDGE: I said I have a contempt for history.

VIDLER: Yes, but it doesn't do you credit to say so. We disagree about it, don't pretend we agree.

MUGGERIDGE: Anyway they arrived in Antioch when it was a living part of history.

VIDLER: Yes, quite a big, important city.

MUGGERIDGE: They went first, as usual, to the synagogue. It's one of the wonderful things of the whole message that Paul had from Christ that, from the crucifixion itself, no man can ever be anything but mortal and all he can ever hope to be or achieve or fulfil is through his relationship to God and that alone.

VIDLER: Absolutely, yes.

MUGGERIDGE: We agree on that if not on history!

VIDLER: Yes certainly.

★　　★　　★

MUGGERIDGE: It was here at this little port of Kavalla in northern Greece that Paul first landed in Europe. Then to Neapolis in Macedonia. What an enterprise it was! From here began the conversion of the civilised world because from here he was set for all the great cities of the west and ultimately for Rome, the then capital of the world. It's difficult to think of a comparable arrival. Perhaps on an infinitely lower and more obscure scale, Lenin arriving unknown at the Finland station in Petrograd in 1917. After all, Paul's arrival touched off 2000 years of history, the story of Christendom with all its fantastic and sublime achievements and all its wickedness and terror. And now one feels the impetus is spent. The light has gone out and what we need is another man to land in another port, and make it shine again.

McMothballs
I would have said that Mr Macmillan had a tiny tiny flavour of mothballs about him.

The Gambler

From a film about Dostoevsky made for Canadian Television by Nielsen-Ferns International

Dostoevsky was forced into the habit of retreating abroad when the pressure of his creditors became insupportable. This involved him in frequent stays at German spas such as Wiesbaden, where a casino is provided to relieve the tedium of imbibing large quantities of distasteful medicinal waters. One wonders what the blameless bourgeois dyspeptics going to and from the Kurhaus, or listening to the orchestra in the gardens, made of this crazed-looking, bearded Russian who had come among them.

In his short brilliant novel, *The Gambler*, Wiesbaden and the other spas appear as Roulettenburg, and the hero, Alexis Ivanovich, is drawn irresistibly to the tables as Dostoevsky was. It was not, however, as Alexis Ivanovich explains, just the play's excitement; he wanted the money, wanted it desperately, and wanted it to come to him in this particular way – by sheer chance rather than by work or stratagem or calculation. How strange it is to think of this inspired writer sitting hour after hour, evening after evening, utterly absorbed in the monotonous repetition of *faites vos jeux*, *rien ne va plus*, with the players frenziedly staking their money, at the very last moment changing their minds and pulling some back or piling some more on; then the announcement of the inexorable number at which the little ball has come to rest, and the agonised calculations of winnings and losses.

Dostoevsky said of himself that he carried everything to excess – love and hate, hope and despair, ecstasy and sentimentality; gambling was, for him, the *reductio ad absurdum* of money. Just to get it and lose it on the turn of a wheel! To acquire riches by chance, and then lose them as suddenly and unaccountably! The banker, the speculator, even the prospec-

236

tor for gold, might persuade himself that his cupidity performed some useful service, but gamblers are the monks of greed, dedicated wholly to its service, with the green-baize tables for an altar on which to set out the sacrificial offerings of coins and banknotes. As money loses its value will the cult go on? It's a possibility that Dostoevsky would have enjoyed exploring.

Some of Dostoevsky's most frenetic gambling excesses were associated with the most physical of his love affairs – with Apollinaria Suslova, a student who approached Dostoevsky initially in a mood of awe at his greatness, and then found him – a common campus drama – far from great in bed. She appears in *The Gambler* as a wilful *femme fatale*.

Writing *The Gambler* proved in every sense therapeutic. For financial reasons it had to be completed in twenty-six days, and to achieve this Dostoevsky procured the services of a stenographer – Anna Grigoryevna Snitkina – who turned out to be exceptionally competent and sensible, and in due course became his second and last wife. On their travels in Europe she had to endure one last gambling debauch, and describes in her diary the appalling straits to which it reduced them – the pawning of everything they had, including her wedding ring, at times the actual starvation to which they were subjected, all made worse for Anna because she was going through her first pregnancy. Then, again at Wiesbaden, the mania spent itself as mysteriously as it had begun, and for the last decade of his life, thanks to Anna's quiet competence, steady affection and careful management, Dostoevsky had the peace of mind to produce his great works in relative ease and security.

Planning
Every time people start planning anything, particularly in economics, I know that it'll end in total chaos and insanity.

Editing with 'Punch'

There are few more melancholy occupations in the world than looking over back numbers of *Punch*, especially if you happened to have been Editor at the time. To say that they're unfunny is an understatement. They are utterly unfunny which is strange since at the time one was straining all the while to make them funny. I couldn't wish my worst enemy to have a more dreadful occupation than being employed to make people laugh, especially the English. It's easier in America where people laugh easily. But I took the job on impulse. A great asset was parody which I happen to like very much. We did parodies of the *New Yorker*, *The Economist*, *The Times* – publications that took themselves seriously. It's exactly the same role as the fool in Shakespeare plays – in life and at court – somebody not particularly highly regarded, but who speaks out, indicating that the Emperor is naked. Because the Emperor always is naked; power always is absurd. The great difficulty of the job was that you wanted to satirise what's going on in the world and the people who run the affairs of the world, but discover that they are intrinsically more absurd than anything you can invent. You try, for instance, to be funny about the BBC, which is a pretty easy target, and discover that the BBC is liable to satirise itself – witness a Third Programme talk on the place of the potato in English folklore. You can't easily rival that! The same with those set in authority over us – as, for example, the Archbishop of Canterbury, at the end of the musical *Godspell*, jumping up and shouting 'Long live God!' Most extraordinary! If there's a God, He must be immortal – unlike Archbishops of Canterbury who, perhaps fortunately, are mortal.

The political cartoons were the part of the magazine that interested me most. One that caused a tremendous row at the time was a drawing of Churchill captioned 'Man goeth forth unto his work and to his labour until the evening'; and it depicted him in a very physically derelict condition, as, indeed, was the case. Everybody knew that he'd stayed on as Prime Minister in the postwar government long after he was capable of exercising his functions. Letters poured in. There was the usual bandying about of the words 'bad taste' which always occurs on those occasions, and Churchill himself, as it turned out – I didn't know at the time – was enormously upset. I read, for instance, in the published diaries of his doctor Lord Moran, of how he found Churchill in an acute state of distress over this cartoon. 'There's malice in it,' he said to Moran. 'Look at my hands, look at my hands, I have beautiful hands.' The picture's not very flattering, I admit, but even so . . .

I felt that *Punch* at that time carried no political clout at all, but this particular case made an impact because people made a row. It's arguable, perhaps, that the row itself led to the Tories summoning up their determination to push Winston out.

Peers and Clergymen

In the days when I first edited Punch, *peers and clergymen were our absolute standby. Whenever I read that there was a threat of closing the House of Lords, or that the number of Church of England ordinands was falling, my heart used to sink, because I thought if they fell beyond a certain point, and if the House of Lords were to shut down, we might as well pack up. We have cherished these two categories of relatively educated individuals, and then given them nothing whatever to do, thereby ensuring a ready supply of eccentricity. Now, is this to continue? Because I notice certain alarming signs. In the first place, in the Upper House they're beginning to suggest that Noble Lords should do things, and that of course is very, very frightening. As for the clergymen, apart from their numbers dwindling, there is also a certain tendency among them to take their religion seriously. Now, as Editor of* Punch, *I could not but feel that this could cut the ground from under our feet, and I hope it won't go any further than it has!*

Steeples and Gargoyles

Humour is the opposite face of mysticism. That's why on cathedrals the steeple climbs into the sky, and the little grinning gargoyle looks down at the earth. They are both saying the same thing – that man is an inadequate creature.

Humour is an expression in grotesque terms of the disparity between human aspiration and human performance. No human activity illustrates that disparity better than sex, which is why sex is so enormously funny. What's more, as you approach the end of your life it gets funnier and funnier.

The curse of the world is pride and humour destroys pride, so the proud detest humour. Shakespeare puts it very well in King John *when he makes the King speak of 'that idiot laughter hateful to our purpose'.*

Bad humour is an evasion of reality; good humour is an acceptance of it.

Humour is the only thing about which the English are completely serious.

Evelyn Waugh

ROBERT ROBINSON: Among those who were the victims of Evelyn Waugh's critical impersonations were Malcolm Muggeridge and Peter Quennell. In his letters Quennell was referred to by Waugh – who uses the manner of a gent who doesn't have to be witty rather than that of a writer who does – as 'fuddy-duddy fish face' and was continually accused of getting above himself. And Malcolm Muggeridge displeased Waugh by presuming to belong to his Club and actually having the rank of Major. 'Margaret's glass eye was washed away at Porto Fino,' Waugh writes, 'so she was spared the sight of Muggeridge.' Now tell me, Malcolm, why didn't he like you?

MUGGERIDGE: I think it's awfully difficult to say why someone doesn't like you because secretly in one's heart of hearts one thinks it's just because they've got bad taste, doesn't one? His fantasy life as an upper-class country gentleman was something that was easy to ridicule, and I often did. I remember thinking that he and Orwell were like two clowns playing opposite each other, because Orwell used to dress up very ostentatiously as a proletarian in the passionate desire that governed his life not to be recognised as an Etonian. He wore loose corduroy bags, not actually tied up with string but they might easily have been. And Waugh dressed up as a country gentleman in enormous broad checks. The two of them based their wardrobe largely on back numbers of *Punch*, I think, more than on life.

ROBINSON: Do you think that Waugh took offence that you both infringed the middle-class pastures that he'd invaded?

QUENNELL: Yes, there is a touch of that. He was prepared to make many excuses both for the members of the upper class and for fellow Catholics. His snobbery and his general antagonism was never in evidence when he was with his fellow believers; he was extremely generous to them and put up with all kinds of people that he wouldn't have done in other circumstances.

MUGGERIDGE: I agree. He was absolutely sincere about his religion. His life was a sort of masquerade that he'd invented himself, and he dressed the part, spoke the part, and I think that as the years rolled by it bored him more and more. But one of the terrible things about embarking on a masquerade is that you can't get out of it, and I think that broke his heart.

The account of his breakdown in his book *The Ordeal of Gilbert Pinfold* is extraordinarily interesting and purely auto-biographical; that's exactly what happened to him. In his breakdown he heard all these voices pointing accusing fingers at him. It's a unique piece of writing in which, in a sense, he was confessing in public, and it's stamped on my mind because, inevitably, there was a Foyles lunch to launch it and I was the Chairman. Waugh was there and it was when he was never without an enormous old-fashioned ear trumpet – I don't think he was in the least deaf actually. As I got up and cleared my throat to undertake the grisly ordeal of making a speech, he very ostentatiously took the ear trumpet out of his ear and put it on the desk in front of him. This raised an enormous laugh which gave me a difficult start.

I think there was also, in some mysterious way, a saintly Evelyn – someone who wanted to be a saint very badly and who kept on, therefore, tumbling into being the opposite.

QUENNELL: There was one virtue I would like to mention. He had extraordinary physical courage. His Commanding Officer during the war, Robert Laycock, told me he'd literally never seen a braver man and that Evelyn's displays of courage just made his hair stand on end.

MUGGERIDGE: I believe he would have been quite glad to have been killed in the war.

QUENNELL: I think he had a strong death wish –

MUGGERIDGE: – because he was living this fantasy life. It's unbearable for human beings to be imprisoned in fantasy, and if the person creates his own fantasy he can't escape; it's a terrible predicament.

Aged Pleasures

The advantages of old age are colossal. First of all, you get rid of an enormous amount of junk. You get rid of ambition – what a boring thing that is! You don't totally get rid of lechery, but a good solid part of it. You have a most delightful feeling of irresponsibility: for instance, you might open The Times, *and you see a formidable article, we'll say, on the Channel Tunnel, and you think to yourself, 'I needn't read it because it does not affect me in any way'. So you're let off an enormous amount of tedious reading, tedious talk. And you have, strangely enough, an additional sharpened sense of what a delightful place the world is, and how enchanting are your fellow human beings. Quite illogical – maybe it's just because you're going to leave them.*

And secondly, perhaps the most agreeable of all, I've got nine grandchildren, and I find their company absolutely enchanting. Whether that's because I am rapidly relapsing into second childhood, and so I'm at one with them, or whether it's just a feeling that they're beginning their pilgrimage through the world and I'm just ending it, but it is the most delightful experience. So whatever you do, get some grandchildren and you'll be all right.

Transmigration

MUGGERIDGE: *The prospect of ending one's days in this world is only like a butterfly shaking itself free of its chrysalis and flying into the sky.*

HAROLD EVANS: *Malcolm may float like a butterfly but he stings like a bee.*

Orbits

There was a famous humorist who said that when he woke up in the morning he always turned to the Obituaries in The Times, *and if he wasn't in them, he got up. I, too, when reading a newspaper, turn immediately to the Obituaries. They make my day and I find them fascinating to write. There's nothing more uplifting and refreshing than typing out: 'We deeply regret to announce the demise . . .' of some scurvy politician in full cry at the moment. I used to believe that when you wrote someone's obituary you might shorten his life, but experience has taught me that you're more likely to extend it indefinitely.*

Courtiers
Garter King-at-Arms! I'd almost rather be Editor of The Times.

246

Panorama Days

In those early days of *Panorama* in the 1950s it used to call itself 'A Window on the World', but it's always strange to me that these studios have no windows. They're completely and utterly cut off, isolated from the world, and I feel that they are places of fantasy not connected with life.

In those days you would have four programme items in the studio, and you had to move from one to the other and not be noticed. I kept on getting it wrong, walking across shot or getting into the wrong set, and it was quite disastrous. I've never been much good at it. But it was an interesting adventure.

It's all a rather confused memory, because quite often there'd be somebody suddenly produced at the last minute. For instance, I remember a surgeon was produced who'd just separated two Siamese twins, and I was completely flummoxed as to what to say to him. I didn't know anything about Siamese twins. So I said, 'Supposing the twins wanted it, could you join them up again?' which was regarded as rather bad taste.

And there was the now historic interview with Brendan Behan when he was in an advanced state of intoxication, quite unable to speak, and it was suggested that we'd better cancel it. But it was very difficult in those days, because it was all live, and Leonard Miall, who was in charge, with great reluctance gave the go ahead. As I left him to go on to the set, I heard him saying to me: 'And if he uses the word,' and he referred to the female genital organ, 'if he uses that word, don't smile.' It's not a word I'd fall into fits of laughter about, or smile at, if I heard it; but such was my only directive, and Behan of course couldn't utter at all. Not even that word. I had to conduct the interview without any help from him. It ran like this: 'Well, I believe that in this play that you've got on, *The Quare Fellow*, the prison scenes are actually based on your experiences in Brixton prison.' He'd make incomprehensible noises, and I'd say, 'Oh well, that's very interesting, and the governor of the prison, I believe, was also . . .' and so on. We managed to stagger on. And then I remembered that sometimes when people are very drunk they can sing when they can't speak. So I said: 'There is that little song in your play, couldn't you perhaps sing it?' And in a very little piping voice he managed to sing it. The final pay-off in itself was comical, because the producer of the play out at Stratford, Joan Littlewood, told me they'd been unable to interest anyone in the West End but that after he appeared drunk on television two West End managers rang up to say they were interested in *The Quare Fellow*. In a very civil way, when he referred to the incident, he always added that it absolutely made his career as a dramatist.

I remember being confronted with Salvador Dali, and finding it very difficult to think what to say to him. So I fell back on asking him whether, when he went to bed, his moustache stayed up or did it subside? And I must say, I think he was much more interested in talking about his moustache than about his art.

One interview that stands out in my mind, not as funny but as oddly poignant, was with Bertrand Russell. We were on some New Year's Day show and he took a very pessimistic attitude to the forthcoming year. I said to him: 'After all, I too take a pessimistic view, but the reason I'm so pessimistic is largely because a great many people have mistakenly accepted your ideas. Yet now you're complaining that the world is going to pieces.' He said that was because the world hadn't adopted his ideas, and the war had disrupted everything. I've always felt a curious sense of hostility, and at the same time a kind of pity for him. Whenever we met, we argued and insulted one another, yet I think there was a kind of mutal sympathy. And when I read his memoirs I realised that he was a person who could have moved in a quite different direction but somehow he'd got misplaced. He hated religion, and yet I think he hated it in the same way that people hate some woman who won't accept them. He hated it because he couldn't reach it – I think he actually felt very drawn to it.

Human Frailty
What Christ had to say was too simple to be grasped, too truthful to be believed. Our faculties are like those smelting works which can only take ore of a high degree of impurity. When the light is too bright we can't see.

Brothelyser
On television I feel like a man playing a piano in a brothel; every now and again he solaces himself by playing 'Abide with Me' in the hope of edifying both the clients and the inmates.

Fly in the Royal Ointment

On 19 October 1957 an article for a top American magazine appeared under the title 'Do We Really Need a Queen? by Malcolm Muggeridge.' It provoked nationwide controversy back home.

It's very difficult for me now to believe that the terrific row over my article in the fifties on the Royal Family really took place. It even surprised me at the time because I'd written, some months before, almost exactly the same thing in slightly different form in the *New Statesman*, and nobody had taken any particular notice of it – which goes to show one of the points of journalism, which is that it's not so much what you write, as when you write it and where you write it. The article was for the *Saturday Evening Post*, then the leading American magazine, and they naturally used it when the Queen was visiting America. They put a title on it which wouldn't have been my choice – 'Do We Really Need a Queen?' Actually, the theme of my article was that we do; that the monarchy is a very useful institution, but it could go very wrong if the encumbent came to be seen as intrinsically very remarkable, very beautiful or a very inspiring person. The only importance the encumbent really has is that she is Queen. She is the ceremonial Head of a State – at that time of an Empire too, which was, I argued in the article, a far better arrangement than, say, having an elected President or Head of State. The Monarch has the same sort of role as a priest, who celebrates Mass and gives out the Blessed Sacrament, thereby becoming a mystical person, but only because he has that particular role. In actual fact he's probably a very ordinary person, and if you were to say that priests have to be mystics, then you wouldn't have very many. Similarly, officers in the army – you don't salute or obey an officer because he's a remarkable person, but because he has the role of an officer.

250

The row was really quite extraordinary. I suppose, if you look it up, you'd find there was a shortage of lead stories at that time – and that's another factor in journalism that has to be taken account of. I was blackguarded in a way that it's difficult now to realise could ever have happened. It was a useful experience in a way. Having been a relatively popular person, you suddenly find yourself absolutely the opposite. And you also realise that the Establishment can mount an attack on an individual with tremendous ferocity, and you have really no means of responding effectively. Individuals responded to the Establishment lead by sending enormous numbers of very rude letters, while my wife Kitty was much embarrassed by abusive telephone calls. Not a single one of these people had read the article, or really knew what was in it. They only knew of the manner in which it had been presented. I remember walking along the front at Brighton, and a man deliberately came across and spat at me – a very interesting experience. Then the National Front came and painted a lot of slogans on my house. As a matter of fact they made a mistake, and first of all painted them on someone else's house. When they found out, they then came and painted them on my house. Another incident was peculiarly horrible; our youngest son was killed in a skiing accident, and someone wrote my wife a letter, very beautifully typed on fine paper, saying she was so very pleased that this death had taken place, and it was very appropriate. That doesn't hurt one really because it's too pathetic and sad, but you wonder how people could put something like that on paper. But they do.

The only feedback I had from the Palace itself was from a great friend of mine, Lord Longford, a very delightful but also somewhat eccentric person. When he was made a Knight of the Garter, being the most important person to be gartered, at the luncheon afterwards he sat next to the Queen. Recounting the incident to me, he said he felt he owed it to our friendship to say to her: 'You know, Ma'am, Malcolm Muggeridge is really quite a nice chap.' I asked him how the Queen responded. 'She looked thoughtful,' he said.

Against the Stream

Once, when I was in great public disfavour, standing in the lobby of a Manchester hotel, a man came up, shook me by the hand and said: 'Never forget that only dead fish swim with the stream.' It's a good saying. If I ever had occasion to have a family crest or motto, I should choose 'Only dead fish swim with the stream'.

A Nod and a Wink

I once asked Lord Chandos in a television interview: 'Tell me now, you're a figure of the Establishment,. how does it really work?' And he said: 'I'll tell you exactly. Somebody rings me up and says, "Oliver, we're thinking of X for post Y", and I say, "Mm, yes?" They understand exactly what I mean.'

Deadly Art

I feel very frightened indeed, and more than that, exceedingly sorry that I ever agreed to become a waxwork, for I have been told since that if the public grow weary of your presence, or if Tussaud's get offended with you, they melt you down, and build up a more popular fellow out of your dripping!

A Twentieth-Century Testimony

A film made with the Evangelical Broadcasting Station for Dutch television

When one is nearing the end of a life, as I am, my allotted span of three score years and ten already passed, hair white and disappearing, breath short, eyes dim, grunting, coughing, groaning, with many other intimations of mortality in flesh and mind and spirit, it's natural enough to be thinking about death. Particularly in the graveyard where my father lies buried, with a space beside him which I expect to be occupying quite soon now. Dust to dust, as the burial service in the Book of Common Prayer puts it.

From my earliest years I've been much given to thinking about death, some would think abnormally, or even morbidly. First, as an infinitely remote and mysterious prospect; then, as the years passed, as an actual happening which must in due course befall me; and now, near-at-hand – so near that it quite cancels out all the plans and expectations and hopes relating to the world that have occupied my mind. As Dr Johnson said of the man expecting to be hanged, the prospect of death wonderfully concentrates the mind.

This might seem in contemporary terms a melancholy, if not unmentionable, case to be in, death having replaced sex as the great taboo, the dirty little secret. I, on the contrary, find it very uplifting; like the close of a June day – a distillation, as it were, of everything most beautiful and most loving in what has gone before. A beginning, not an end; the darkness falling, and in the sky, a distant glow, the lights of St Augustine's City of God. Looking towards them, I say over to myself John Donne's splendid words: 'Death, thou shalt die.' Here, in the graveyard, the dust settles; there, in the

City of God, eternity begins.

> 'O that thou shouldst give dust a tongue
> To cry to thee.'

So writes George Herbert: words with a beginning and an end, expressing what never began and cannot end. Yet the passion to speak persists. Like seeing someone off on a train, and, as the train begins to move, rushing along with it to get in one last word.

It is often said that old age is a sort of second childhood. And it's true in a way. More often than not, yesterday is totally obliterated, but I can recall exactly happenings as long as fifty or sixty years ago. It is the same with places. Natural scenes, like the lovely Sussex fields; the sheep, the orchard, the sky – again, it's like the child's sharp reaction, as if I were seeing the place for the first time, although in fact I see them almost every day. And then with people, too. As a child, one has the same sort of relationship with everyone; they are all uncles and aunts, brothers and sisters, belonging to one family, and so to be trusted, to be loved and to be confided in. So, when people see this second childhood as an intimation of senescence, I don't agree. I am more inclined to think of it as a conditioning process for eternity; as accustoming one to the circumstances that one is going to move into; and furthermore, as bearing out those sayings of Jesus about how we have to be like a little child to understand His words and to enter His kingdom.

There is another thing that happens to me nowadays quite often. It sounds rather strange, but actually it is enormously delightful. And that is a vivid sense of being half in and half out of my body, as though it were almost a toss-up whether I went back into my body and resumed my earthly life, or made off, leaving my battered old carcase behind me for ever. In this curious state, in a sort of limbo between time and eternity, I have a conviction, stronger than I can possibly convey, that as an infinitesimal particle of life, I am a participant in our Creator's purposes, which are loving and not malign, creative and not destructive, universal and not particular; and in that conviction a very great comfort and a very great joy. Of course, in such a state of mind one looks back on one's life with a sort of distaste, as though it was so much wasted time. On the other hand, I must admit that the profession of journalism, which I have practised for the last half century and more, has one very great advantage in giving one a very sharp sense indeed of the sheer buffoonery of power and of those who seek it and exercise it.

Without a God, men have to be gods themselves and fabricate their own immortality; as we see in wax, in Madame Tussaud's Exhibition, a place of images. In the beginning was the image, and the image became wax, and dwelt among us, full of absurdity. Images of the famous and infamous dead, of the celebrated and notorious living. Above all, of the gods and goddesses of the media – these images of images, programmed to shout and gesticulate in accordance with their preordained roles. Even, come to that, an image of myself.

From time to time, I have a bizarre notion that I might change places with my image and spend a few quiet days in Marylebone Road, leaving my image to do the various things that I have got to do. I like very much Pascal's notion that people in authority need to dress up to justify their position of eminence. If judges didn't wear ermine, Pascal says, who could possibly suppose that they were capable of dispensing true justice? Likewise, priests in vestments, scholars in gowns, admirals in gold braid and generals in red tabs, kings and queens with their crowns and their orbs, and chefs with their tall white hats. In the same sort of way, clowns have to paint their faces in order that people may know they are being funny. In other words, authority requires an image. Men in relation to power become images; it is only in relation to God that they dare to be men.

There they all are in Madame Tussaud's Exhibition, the captains and the kings, the great ones who ebb and flow with the moon – all in wax. Kings and queens, presidents and politicians, soldiers and sailors, pontiffs and ideologues – all waxworks with their names written on water, or, in contemporary terms, on a television screen; all stars in an interminable soap opera called history. I've always had a feeling, from my very earliest memories, that somehow, somewhere, there was another dimension of reality where the fancy dress was put aside, the grease paint was washed off, the arc lamps were lowered. Even as a child, if I happened to catch a glimpse of a mayor in his regalia, or a vicar in his, it filled me with a kind of wonder. As it might a child looking incredulously at a Father Christmas with a cotton-wool beard.

I feel as though all my life I've been looking for an alternative scene; for the face behind the cotton wool, the flesh beneath the wax, the light beyond the arc lamps, time beyond the ticking of the clocks, and a vista beyond the furthermost reach of mortal eyes even when magnified across innumerable light years, for a destiny beyond history. How extraordinary that I should have found it, not, like Icarus, in flying up to the sun, but in God coming down to me – in the Incarnation.

Lights Out
I have a strange feeling now as I approach the end of my life that it'll end in a studio with the voice of the director saying 'CUT' – and out go the lights – and out go I!